Learning Quartz Composer

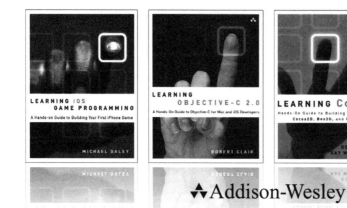

Learning Quartz Composer

A Hands-On Guide to Creating Motion Graphics with Quartz Composer

Graham Robinson

Surya Buchwald

✦✦Addison-Wesley

Upper Saddle River, NJ • Boston • Indianapolis • San Francisco
New York • Toronto • Montreal • London • Munich • Paris • Madrid
Capetown • Sydney • Tokyo • Singapore • Mexico City

Many of the designations used by manufacturers and sellers to distinguish their products are claimed as trademarks. Where those designations appear in this book, and the publisher was aware of a trademark claim, the designations have been printed with initial capital letters or in all capitals.

The authors and publisher have taken care in the preparation of this book, but make no expressed or implied warranty of any kind and assume no responsibility for errors or omissions. No liability is assumed for incidental or consequential damages in connection with or arising out of the use of the information or programs contained herein.

The publisher offers excellent discounts on this book when ordered in quantity for bulk purchases or special sales, which may include electronic versions and/or custom covers and content particular to your business, training goals, marketing focus, and branding interests. For more information, please contact:

U.S. Corporate and Government Sales
(800) 382-3419
corpsales@pearsontechgroup.com

For sales outside the United States, please contact:

International Sales
international@pearson.com

Visit us on the Web: informit.com/aw

Library of Congress Cataloging-in-Publication Data

Robinson, Graham, 1982–
  Learning quartz composer : a hands-on guide to creating motion graphics with Quartz composer / Graham Robinson, Surya Buchwald.
        p. cm.
  Includes index.
  ISBN 978-0-321-85758-3 (pbk. : alk. paper)
  1. Computer animation. 2. Digital video. 3. Quartz (Electronic resource) I. Buchwald, Surya, 1982- II. Title.
  TR897.7.R595 2012
  777'.7--dc23

                                           2012015316

Copyright © 2013 Pearson Education, Inc.

ISBN-13: 978-0-321-85758-3
ISBN-10:   0-321-85758-5
Text printed in the United States on recycled paper at Courier in Westford, Massachusetts.
First printing, July 2012

Editor in Chief
Mark Taub

Acquisitions Editor
Trina MacDonald

Development Editor
Sheri Cain

Managing Editor
John Fuller

Project Editor
Anna Popick

Copy Editor
Jill Hobbs

Indexer
John S. (Jack) Lewis

Proofreader
Diane Freed

Publishing Coordinator
Olivia Basegio

Multimedia Developer
Dan Scherf

Cover Designer
Chuti Prasertsith

Compositor
Rob Mauhar

I would like to acknowledge Jesus as my inspiration and the source of my creativity and talent. My wife Natalie, my muse and the most caring, supportive, fun human I have ever met, thank you so much! My father Bruce, without your support and encouragement I never would have been able to become self-employed and start this whole journey.
—Graham

I dedicate this book to my Mom for always telling me to do what I love (it's working!), to my Dad for instilling in me a talent and love for the arts, and to my Grandma Theda for getting us our first computer when I was but a wee lad, giving a jump-start to my tech education. Thanks to my friends in Stargaze and LAVA for encouraging and believing in me when I had the crazy idea to get into making interactive ridiculousness.
—Surya

Contents at a Glance

Contents

Preface

Welcome to *Learning Quartz Composer*! We guarantee this will be the most fun geek book you have read, and by the end your digital world will be a better-looking place. Whether you dream of live visuals, interactive installations, Cocoa apps, dashboard widgets, or extra awesomeness for your film and motion graphics projects, Quartz Composer will enable you to develop beautiful solutions in amazingly short periods of time.

With the introduction of Quartz Composer in Mac OS X Tiger, Apple delivered a very powerful and unique tool, and with each operating system upgrade it becomes better and better. Quartz Composer is like your graphics card's special sauce; hidden away on your Developer Tools disk, it's your Mac's best kept secret.

Creating with Quartz Composer is superfast because it is a live, constantly rendering environment. Thus, if you make a change, you will see the result immediately, rather than having to wait for RAM previews or long renders. In performance environments, a Quartz Composer file can take live inputs from music or cameras, allowing for unique interaction and improvisation. Another massive advantage is that you don't ever have to define your project dimensions, so you can work on them freely and later choose to output a video file to devices ranging from a tiny phone screen to a high-definition video editing program.

So if Quartz Composer is so great, why isn't everyone using it? Well, there is a little bit more to the story. Quartz Composer is a graphical programming environment, which sounds scary enough to make most creative types run for the hills. When you add in an unusual (though highly usable) interface, you can see why it has remained in the dark. Fear not—we will break it all down into plain English and give you the confidence to do anything you want with this handy tool.

This book launches you directly into building and manipulating beautiful compositions. Each concept is introduced as part of a hands-on project, with video tutorial, steadily building your "qc-fu" and demonstrating/encouraging experimentation every step of the way. The projects start out very simple, and the first focus is always on beautiful visual feedback, so you know why you are learning what you are learning and want to explore the systems they are creating.

Audience for This Book

With only the very basics of computer literacy, this book/DVD combination launches the unsophisticated user into creating art projects, visuals for a band or party, wild screensavers, and RSS-powered trade-show kiosks. For anyone with a programming background, the material quickly opens up a new world of visual potential.

Who Should Read This Book

The target audience for this book consists of Maker types: people who are delighted and excited by projects that enable them to create new things from what they have, but who need a helping hand to get them going. The nature of Quartz Composer means that its appeal spans many genres. Motion graphics designers, filmmakers, VJs, artists, interactive programmers, and Cocoa developers—all can learn something here that will apply to their jobs tomorrow.

Who Shouldn't Read This Book

If you are an advanced Quartz Composer user looking for detailed knowledge about using GLSL and OpenCL in Quartz Composer or creating your own plugins in Objective-C Quartz Composer, this book may be a little too basic. However, even a long-time Quartz Composer user could benefit from some of the tips and tricks we've discovered on our own learning journeys.

We'd Like to Hear from You

This book is about your experimentation, and we expect great things from you, so please drop in and share what you have created. You will also be able to access any updates, download the book's projects, and more at this site: http://iloveqc.org.

As a reader of this book, you are our most important critic and commentator. We value your opinion and want to know what we're doing right, what we could do better, which areas you'd like to see us publish in, and any other words of wisdom you're willing to pass our way.

When you write to the publisher, please be sure to include this book's title and the names of the authors, as well as your name, phone, and/or email address. The editor will carefully review your comments and share them with the authors and others who have worked on this book. Please note that due to the volume of email we cannot respond to all inquiries/comments.

Email: trina.macdonald@pearson.com

Mail: Trina MacDonald
          Senior Acquisitions Editor, Addison-Wesley
          Pearson Education, Inc.
          1249 8th Street
          Berkeley, CA 94710 USA

For more information about Pearson Education books or conferences, see our website at: http://iloveqc.org.

Organization of This Book

There are 14 chapters in this book, each of which builds on the last, transforming you from total beginner to Quartz Composer Ninja. The book is divided into two parts: Part I teaches the basics of how the different tools or patches can be used and Part II builds on what you have learned to make more advanced compositions.

Part I: Quartz Beginner

- **Chapter 1, "What Is Quartz Composer and Why Should I Learn It?"** This chapter introduces Quartz Composer, explaining what it is and how it can be used. It describes the range of outputs—Quartz file, movie, screensaver, and so on. The emphasis here is on flexibility and encouragement for the reader to experiment at every stage.

- **Chapter 2, "The Interface and Playing a Movie."** This chapter covers the very basics of Quartz Composer launching it, the layout of the interface, and the concept of the Quartz Composer Editor versus a traditional "what you see is what you get" (WYSIWYG) program.

- **Chapter 3, "Adding Visual Effects (Pimping It Out)."** Quartz Composer comes with a variety of built-in image filters for effects. It's easy to start routing your graphics and video through these filters, but some quirks and caveats that pop up could easily frustrate you. This chapter introduces the different types of effects available and the tools you'll need to come to grips with them.

- **Chapter 4, "Using LFOs, Interpolation, and Trackballs to Move Stuff."** One of the important concepts of the book is teaching you to create beautiful organic motion; Chapter 4 describes the tools you need to do so. The best part of the lesson is that all of these tools can work together and allow you to control many different things, from size to positioning to color. Trackballs and the **3D Transformation** patches help you control which part of your virtual world you are looking at.

- **Chapter 5, "Debugging (When Things Go Wrong)."** With the power of experimentation in Quartz Composer comes the inevitable "What did I do wrong?" moments. There are some helpful patches to get users through these tough times.

- **Chapter 6, "Particles (Little Flying Bits of Bling)."** This chapter explains what particles are, along with Quartz Composer's **Particle System** patch and how to use it to make cool stuff like rain and fire. You can even use an image or movie as the particle! A brief introduction to blend modes for layering images and video together is provided as well.

- **Chapter 7, "Mouse Input (Making Your Mouse Do Cool Stuff)."** The mouse is an excellent input device for interactive work, and most computers will have one (or else a trackpad). In this chapter, we teach you how to put the mouse to work inside Quartz Composer.

- **Chapter 8, "MIDI Interfacing (Getting Sliders and Knobs Involved)."** MIDI controllers have historically been used to control audio software and hardware. With Quartz Composer, you can now use keyboards, drum machines, and banks of sliders and knobs to control visual images.

- **Chapter 9, "Interacting with Audio (Get Stuff Grooving to the Beat)."** Now that you have an understanding of the use of LFOs, the mouse, and MIDI, the concept of using audio processing to control values within compositions can be easily introduced. Initially, ways to manipulate the volume peak and microphone input are demonstrated for a quick "Wow" factor, but then we move on to splitting the spectrum, using smooth and math functions to enhance the aesthetics of the application. In addition, we cover how to export your compositions as normal movie files.

- **Chapter 10, "Lighting and Timelines (The Dark Side of QC)."** This chapter introduces the topic of lighting, including all settings that a computer light has but the light in your room doesn't. Experimentation with light, its positioning and its strength, and getting other controller objects involved are encouraged. Those readers who are used to normal editing and motion graphics packages will be happy to find out how Quartz Composer's timelines work.

- **Chapter 11, "Replication/Iteration (The Bomb)."** Why have just one interesting interactive object when you can have hundreds? One of the great things about Quartz Composer is that once you have created a single object, you can make hundreds without any of that boring copy-and-paste nonsense!

Part II: Quartz Ninja

- **Chapter 12, "Modeling Complex Environments (3D Cities)."** In this chapter, we take a lot of what you have learned through the earlier chapters and use it to create an awesome audio reactive city scene. Readers learn how to turn cubes into buildings, to create floors, and to create more complex camera moves.

- **Chapter 13, "Create a Cocoa App (Send Quartz to Your Friends)."** Apple makes it easy for amateurs to create native applications that can manipulate Quartz Composer compositions. This chapter covers the basics of using Xcode and guides you all the way through publishing an application.

- **Chapter 14, "Create a Screensaver."** Building on the earlier discussions of LFO and interpolation, this chapter uses patch time and random output to demonstrate longer-term, more gradually developing patches. It also explains how to wrap up and install patches as screensavers.

- **Chapter 15, "Secret Patches, Core Image Filters, and GLSL (Pushing the Boundaries)."** Quartz provides a rich feature set and many objects for developing stunning compositions. Beyond its own capabilities, many interesting and exciting possibilities are provided by third-party plugins, access to the shader language GLSL, Core Image filters, and OpenCL. This chapter introduces the plugins included with Quartz Composer, including how to install them, how to access Kineme's work, and how to make your own Core Image filter.

Tutorial Videos and DVD Resources

With the book comes a great DVD, complete with a video tutorial for each chapter. The book and tutorials work together, so you can see exactly how to accomplish the more tricky bits covered in the book. The DVD also includes sample projects for each chapter, as well as some images we refer to in the chapters. Enjoy!

Acknowledgments

This book has been a lot of fun to write and simply would not have happened without a lot of time, effort, and help from these fantastic people:

- Our first editor at Addison-Wesley, Chuck Toporek, and his superstar assistant, Romny French. Chuck found our online video tutorials and made this all happen. Chuck and Romny were succeeded by editor Trina MacDonald and assistant Olivia Basegio, who helped us make it over the finish line. Without everyone's support, guidance, and encouragement, we would never have been able to become authors.

- Dr. Monica Schraefel, Dr. Mike Poppelton, and Dr. Eric Cooke at Southampton University, who opened up the world of computer science to me (Graham) and allowed me the freedom to explore the more creative sides of it.

About the Authors

Graham Robinson runs Shakinda Productions in Belfast, Ireland, specializing in innovative projection design and interactive visual systems creation. He believes that technology allows us to create art that can inspire humanity and transform society, and has performed audio-visual sets as VJ Shakinda worldwide.

Surya Buchwald runs MMMLabs in Portland, Oregon, creating interactive experiences for Nike, Intel, Scion, and others. He traverses the globe as the VJ for The Glitch Mob, bringing the Quartz Composer magic to fans all over. He also creates interactive video instruments and performs with them as Momo the Monster.

Part I

Quartz Beginner

Chapter 1

What Is Quartz Composer and Why Should I Learn It?

Welcome to the first chapter! Are you ready to discover a whole new world? This chapter introduces Quartz Composer, explains how it differs from other applications you may have used before, and describes the many different end products you can create with it. We'll explain just how flexible it is and why you should always experiment, experiment, experiment!

Play Video Introduction to Quartz Composer

Still not really sure what Quartz Composer is? Quartz Composer (QC) is a node-based graphical programming language. If that sounds complex, it simply means that you will be connecting boxes with squiggly lines instead of editing a timeline or using a drawing tool (see Figure 1.1). QC allows you to build up things—for example, you can take a QuickTime video, pass it through a filter, combine it with shapes, and display that on the screen. It takes some getting used to, but between reading this book and viewing its DVD, you'll be a QC ninja in no time.

Figure 1.1   Quartz Composer interface versus Photoshop and Final Cut Pro

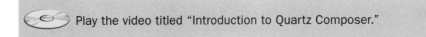

Play the video titled "Introduction to Quartz Composer."

If you haven't done so already, pop in the DVD and check out a few examples to see what's possible with Quartz Composer.

At this stage, if you haven't already set up Quartz Composer, you need to get it on your machine. This is a painless process, but it will involve digging out your original Mac install disks, (or rocking over to Mac dev at http://developer.apple.com, setting up an account, and downloading the installer).

Installing and Setting Up Quartz Composer

 Play the video titled "Installing and Setting Up Quartz Composer."

Follow these steps to install Quartz Composer:

1. Grab your Snow Leopard or Leopard Install DVD and stick it in your Mac.
2. Browse to Optional Installs > XcodeTools and double-click XcodeTools.mpkg.
3. Step through the installer and restart your machine.
4. Quartz Composer is now installed to Macintosh HD > Developer > Applications > Quartz Composer. If you drag the icon to your dock, it will add a launch shortcut.

Alternatively, if you are running Mac OSX Lion, follow these steps:

1. Open the App Store.
2. Search for "Xcode."
3. Download and step through the installer.
4. Quartz Composer is now installed to Macintosh HD > Developer > Applications > Quartz Composer. If you drag the icon to your dock, it will add a launch shortcut.

Congratulations, you are ready to rock!

Outputs

There are many different ways to output your QC productions (or "compositions," as we'll call them). Most simply, you can share them as Quartz composition files (extension .qtz), which means other people will be able to see exactly how you made your composition and add their own ideas to it—a great choice for collaboration. If you save a Quartz composition to ~/Library/Screen Savers or the /Library/Screen Savers folder, it's ready to be a screensaver and will appear in your Screen Saver Preference Panel (see Figure 1.2).

If you want to include your composition in a webpage or dashboard widget (which load via the same WebKit plugin), use the <embed> tag. (For more information, go to http://developer.apple.com/documentation/GraphicsImaging/Conceptual/QuartzComposer/qc_webkit/chapter_8_section_1.html#//apple_ref/doc/uid/TP40001357-CH3-SW6.)

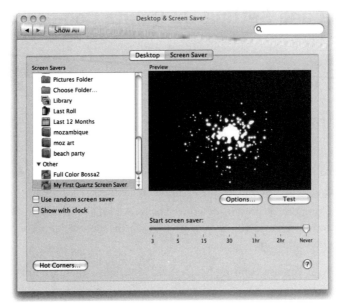

Figure 1.2   Quartz composition as a screensaver

Alternatively, you can export the composition as a QuickTime movie of a specified length and resolution. This method means that anyone with QuickTime installed can watch your composition and, if they have the QuickTime player version 7 or higher, will be able to see any interactive elements of your composition. Once you have the composition formatted as a movie, you can upload it to YouTube or load it into Final Cut, Video Jockey software, or other programs, just like any other movie file.

Not enough for you? Using Cocoa, it's simple to create an application that runs your composition. (See Chapter 13.)

Getting even geekier, you can "publish" certain controls of your compositions so they can be bound with an interface builder to create interfaces for other programs you may have written (http://vidvox.net/wiki/index.php/QuartzComposer_ Adding_a_published_input). The publishing process can also be used in a specific Video Jockey setup with VDMX to create some very powerful live performance experiences.

Surely that's enough—but wait, there's more! Using a QCRenderer class, you can run a QC file in any OpenGL context. If you're not sure what an OpenGL context is, don't panic. . . . I'm covering all the bases here just to show you just how many different ways there are to output your creations from QC.

Flexibility

As you can see, there are many, many different ways to put your QC files to work—but that's only half the story. The range of what you can put in a Quartz composition is also formidable.

QC has an impressive range of filters that come from the core image library. You can have a lot of fun just putting photos, videos, or Photoshop files through a couple of filters. QC can also combine images using 31 different blending modes, some of which Photoshop users will recognize—Add, Alpha, Multiply, and so on—and some they won't—Luminescence Premultiply, anyone?

As well as being a great compositor of images and movies, QC loves live data streams, including audio being picked up by a microphone, RSS feeds from the Internet, MIDI and OSC data from other programs, JavaScript patches within a composition, and data from the ambient light and motion sensors from a MacBook Pro. All of these data streams can be manipulated and represented in incredible visualizations.

Three-dimensional environments can be created; 3D objects loaded, lit, textured, and animated; and camera moves animated on timelines. Lots of smooth and simple controller patches are also built into QC, which allow complex and organic movements to be created simply and quickly.

The possibilities are endless.

Experimentation

This is where you come in: Experiment, experiment, experiment. It is impossible for us, as authors, to highlight all of the possibilities provided by QC. To get the most from QC, you need to take the initiative and play around. Anywhere you see an input to a patch, think, "What could I connect to that?" The beauty of QC is that it's live, so once you have that thought, just noodle out from the closest patch and find out what happens. Then try another hole, a different value, or another controller. Keep going until your composition looks nothing like what it was when you started!

We are expecting some awesome results from you, our apprentices, so in preparation, we created a special site for your creations at `http://www.iloveqc.org`. As soon as you have something that looks a bit different, get your experiments online and let everyone else enjoy them. Share your compositions, learn from others' work, and collaborate. Let the QC explosion begin!

Summary

In this chapter we covered what Quartz Composer is, how to install it, and which kinds of wonderful things you can do with it. We also introduced experimentation as one of the key concepts to help you learn QC: Play around as much as possible and have fun!

Challenges

This chapter described how to install Quartz Composer, so why not start it up and play with some of the templates? If you get stuck, don't worry; just head to Chapter 2, where we will explain how to get started.

Chapter 2

The Interface and Playing a Movie

By now, you realize just how awesome and flexible Quartz Composer is and may already be dreaming up a few masterpieces. You should also have QC set up and ready to go on your machine. This chapter is the beginning of getting your hands dirty and taking your first step to Quartz ninja-dom.

First things first. We'll launch Quartz Composer and explain why what you see isn't always what you get with QC. Then we'll break down the basics of the interface. Finally, the video tutorial will teach you to get a movie playing. Ready? Let's go!

Launching Quartz Composer

Unlike most programs, Quartz Composer doesn't hang out in your Applications folder. Instead, it's kickin' it in Mac HD > Developer > Applications.

The simplest way to launch QC is to browse there and double-click the icon; however, as we are going to be using the program a lot, you'll probably want to make a dock shortcut. To do so, drag the icon to your dock and slip it into position. If you prefer to let Spotlight or Quicksilver launch your apps, a simple "qu" is plenty to get you into the game.

You should now have launched Quartz Composer. On Leopard, click Choose (the default of Blank Composition should be selected); on Tiger, you get a blank composition on launching QC. It should look something like Figure 2.1.

At this moment, it's important to not panic; this is the first test of your Quartz ninja journey, a test of nerve. It's perfectly reasonable to be a little confused about what do to with those boxes and grids. Resist the temptation to flee and go watch TV! You can master the weirdness.

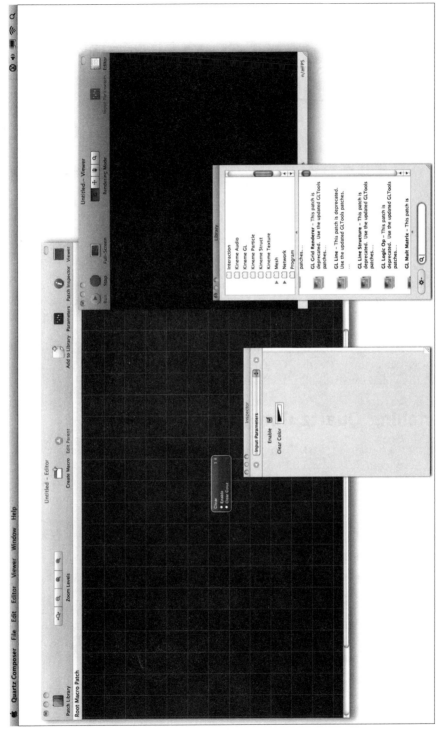

Figure 2.1 The interface for a blank composition (Leopard)

Editor versus WYSISYG

 Play the video titled "Get to Know the Quartz Composer Interface."

What You See Is What You Get (WYSISYG) is how we normally work with programs such as Word or Photoshop. When you press the "a" key, the letter "a" is typed on screen—simple. However, when you launch Quartz Composer, there doesn't appear to be anywhere to type or draw.

Quartz Composer is a visual programming language. That means you add objects and make connections in the dark gray Editor; these changes affect a virtual world, which can be seen with the Viewer (Figure 2.2). If you drag a video file to the Editor, it will appear as a box with the name of that video, but nothing appears in the Viewer (i.e., what you see is not a video).

Although it may be frustrating at first, you will soon learn how to make things show up in the Viewer. Think of the Editor as where you wire circuits and the Viewer as showing you whether the light bulb has come on . . . or the Editor as under the hood of a car and the Viewer as showing you how those changes affect the car's handling . . . or the Editor as where you mix your potions and the Viewer as where the magic happens . . . .

Thus the Editor where you make everything happen. It is where you will connect patches with noodles so that videos go through filters, or do something else. At the top of the blank composition, there are a few buttons: The first button, Patch Library (Leopard: Patch Creator), pops open the Patch Library or brings it to the front, in case it has become hidden behind another window. More on the Patch Library later . . . .

Next, some zoom controls allow you to zoom in and out. Zoom in to make it easier to connect patches, and zoom out to see how various patches link together on bigger compositions.

In the middle of the Editor is the Create Macro button, which allows you to wrap up a few patches you want to use lots of times into one neat patch. Next is Edit Parent, which will be grayed out or disabled at this point. This is another button whose use is explained later.

To the right is Add to Library (Leopard: Create Clip), which is disabled on launch; it allows you to create templates for other compositions from parts or all of the current composition. Next comes Patch Parameters, which, when clicked, opens a drawer to the right of the Editor grid to allow you to change the patch and composition settings. This is neater way of making such changes than using the next button, Patch Inspector, which pops a window to allow you to do the same thing; however, Patch Inspector includes a few extra settings we will need on occasion. More on these two buttons in the section, "Patch Inspector/Patch Variables." The final button, Viewer, opens or brings the Viewer to the front.

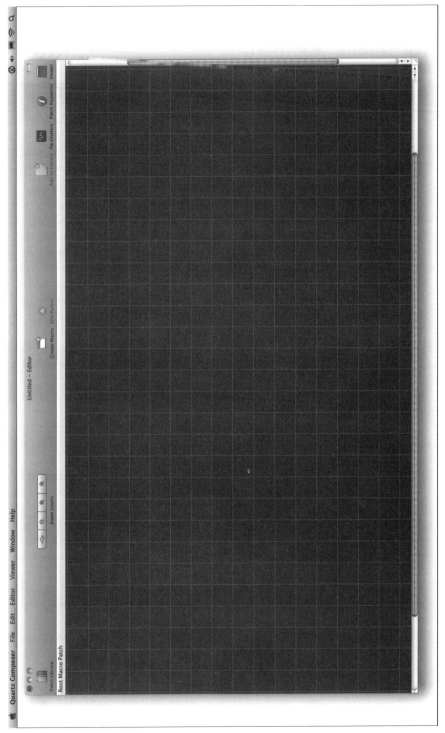

Figure 2.2   Editor Interface pane

Viewer

Figure 2.3 shows your view on the world you have created in your composition; this is what is exported and seen by the world. Put simply, it doesn't matter what's in the Editor—if you can't see it in the Viewer, no one will.

The Viewer toolbar allows you to control how your composition runs. A Quartz composition is normally always running, so the changes you make in the Editor will be seen immediately. If you want to stop the composition's execution, save some computing/battery power, or restart the composition to view some time-based effects from the beginning, you can use the Run and Stop buttons to do so. The Full-Screen option is self-explanatory, but it's worth noting that the Quartz Preferences will allow you to make the mouse invisible while Quartz Composer is in full screen mode.

The Rendering Mode buttons help you with working out a problem or "debugging" (covered in Chapter 5). Input Parameters allows you to edit parts of your composition that you have made interactive or published—more on that in the advanced section. Finally, the Editor button opens or brings to the front of the Editor window the composition you are viewing.

At the bottom of the Viewer, notice the acronym "FPS," which stands for "frames per second." FPS helps you check that your compositions aren't over-straining your Mac. (More on this in Chapter 3.)

In the center of the Viewer is the size of the Viewer window. Quartz Composer works in a virtual space, so the Viewer allows you to place a camera in this virtual space, at the fixed resolution and aspect ratio of a window on your screen. Although the Viewer can be any size and shape, it's helpful to work with the Viewer at the size and aspect ratio (wide-screen or normal TV, 4:3) that match your final output. For learning purposes, just keep the Viewer at a size that lets you see what's going on without getting in the way of the Editor and other panels.

Patch Library (Creator)

Figure 2.4 shows the Patch Library. From here, you select the patches to add to your compositions. The various patches are arranged into groups with short descriptions to help you find the right patch for the right job, so take some time to browse through the library and see what's available. If you click any patch in the list, a longer description appears at the bottom of the Patch Library. To add a patch, drag it with the mouse from the library, double-click it, or, if it's highlighted in the list, press Enter. Using this keyboard shortcut will save you time when you become more familiar with Quartz Composer and use the search feature at the top of the Patch Creator to find specific patches by name.

Using the search feature can also be a good way to explore and experiment with a patch you might have missed. For example, type "image" and you will find a wide range of patches in different categories that relate to images.

Figure 2.3 Viewer pane

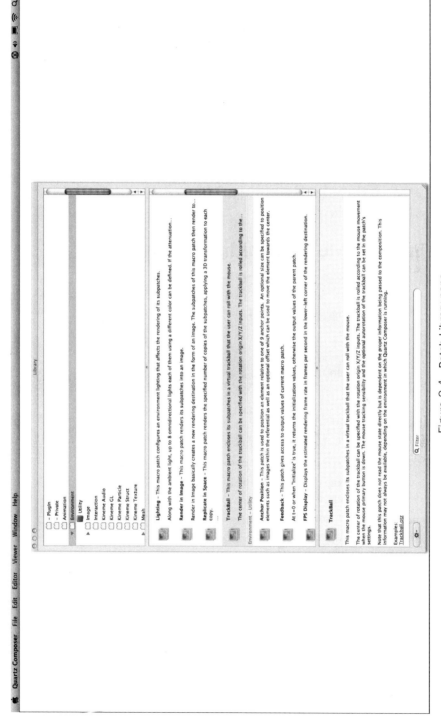

Figure 2.4   Patch Library pane

Patch Inspector/Patch Variables

When you add a patch to the Editor from the Patch Creator, you will notice it has a number of parameters with small circles beside them. These are the important noodle connection points. Mouse over one of these circles, and click and drag out your first noodle. This yellow line, or noodle, allows you to connect patches. As well as adding noodles to change the composition's attributes, you can adjust these properties directly using the Patch Inspector and patch variables (see Figure 2.5). The Patch Inspector is arranged in pages that can be clicked through using the arrows, selected from the drop-down menu, or accessed through a shortcut via ⌘-1, ⌘-2, ⌘-3. The patch variables give you page 2 input parameters, where most of the important settings are found for the majority of patches.

Playing a Movie Tutorial Instructions

So far, we've taken a quick tour of the QC interface. Don't worry if some of the details didn't make sense; after you watch a few video tutorials, everything will become much clearer. Speaking of which, let's get our first movie playing in Quartz!

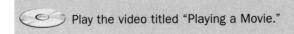
Play the video titled "Playing a Movie."

To play a video, follow these steps:

1. Open a new blank document in Quartz Composer.
2. Drag a movie file from the Finder onto the QC canvas.

   Now the image is generated, but you can't see it yet. To make it visible, we have to render the image.

3. Drag a **Billboard** from the patch list on the left onto the QC canvas.
4. Click and drag from the *Image* output of the **Movie** patch to the *Image* input of the **Billboard** patch.

   In the Viewer, you should now see the movie playing. If you can't see the Viewer, press Shift-⌘-V to bring it up.

   Your movie should now play—but it takes up only half the screen.

5. Hover your mouse over the *Width* input on the **Billboard** patch. You'll see that the width is set to 1.

   This is how QC's coordinate system works. The left side of the screen is –1; the right side is +1 (see Figure 2.6).

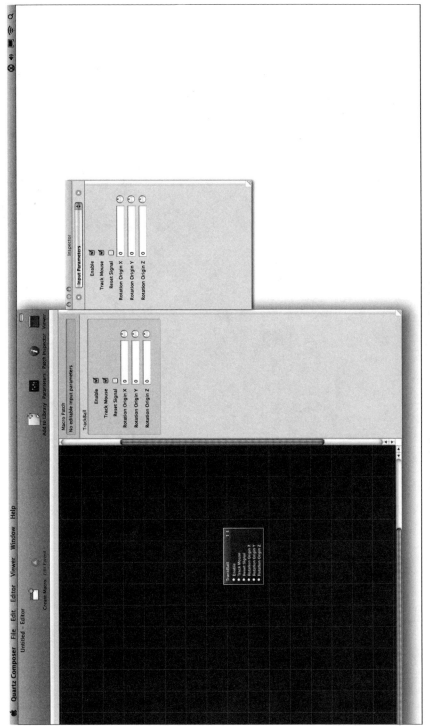

Figure 2.5 Patch properties and Patch Inspector

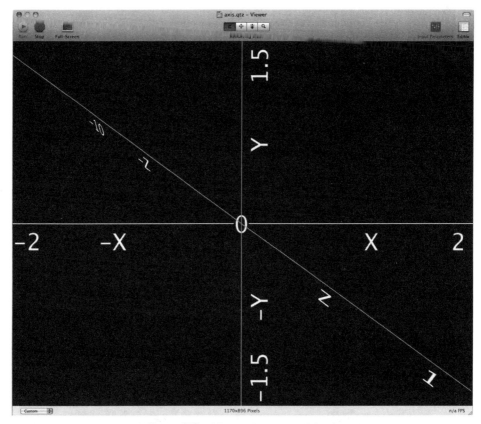

Figure 2.6   3D coordinates explained

6. Click the **Billboard** patch to select it, and then move over to the Inspector window (press ⌘-I if the Inspector is not visible).

7. Click the right-facing arrow to move to page 2 of the Inspector, and then change the value for the **Billboard**'s *Width* to 2 by typing this value.

   Your movie should now stretch edge-to-edge in the Viewer.

8. To understand the way Quartz Composer positions things from –1 to 1, play with the *Width* and *Position* wheels.

Summary

That's all for this chapter. You now understand that working with Quartz Composer is different than working with your average application because it's a graphical programming language. You also understand the basics of its interface and created that all-important first Quartz file—well done!

Challenges

The challenge for this chapter is to get more than one movie playing at once in the Viewer window. Remember that you have control over the size and position of your billboard and over the number of billboards that appear in your composition.

Chapter 3

Adding Visual Effects (Pimping It Out)

Now that you have the know-how to load a movie in Quartz Composer and see it in your Viewer, let's walk through the process of adding effects, such as filters, to your compositions.

 Play the video titled "Make Filter Chains."

Adding a Filter

Quartz Composer comes with a fantastic selection of built-in filters that you can use to manipulate your images. Color filters can modify hue, saturation, luminosity, brightness, and contrast in your images. Geometry and distortion filters can change the shape of your images in precise or organic fashions. There are also filters to tile your images, to blur and sharpen them, to reduce noise, and to do many other things.

In this exercise, you'll add a **Pixellate** filter, which affects the pixel size of the final image. To add a filter, follow these steps:

1. Start a new composition, and get a video playing like you did in Chapter 2 (**Movie Loader** + **Billboard**). The movie must be 640 × 480 pixels in dimensions for this exercise.

2. Use the Patch Library to find the **Pixellate** filter. You can scroll down until you see it, or type "pixel" in the search field and grab it from the resulting shortlist. Make sure to check the "description" panel of the Patch Library, and choose the "Pixellate" choice that "Makes an image blocky." Add the **Pixellate** patch to your composition by dragging it to the composition view.

> **Tip**
>
> In Leopard (OS X 10.5), the Patch Library is called Patch Creator. It works mostly the
> same way, minus some nifty organizational functions and alternative views introduced in
> Snow Leopard. Thankfully, the search box is the same, except that it's located at the top
> of the Patch Creator in Leopard instead of at the bottom of the Patch Library.

3. Connect the *Image* output of your **Movie Loader** to the *Image* input of the
   Pixellate patch.

4. Connect the *Image* output of the **Pixellate** patch to the *Image* input of the
   Billboard patch. Make sure the **Billboard**'s *Width* is set to 2.

   Notice how the original connection from your **Movie** patch to the **Billboard**
   automatically disappears? A Rendering Destination (like the **Billboard**) can
   hold only one image stream at a time, so it is updated to keep you from connecting more than one.

5. You should immediately see a difference in your output window. The movie
   becomes pixellated at the default scale value of 8. Double-click the dot to the left
   of the *Scale* input of the **Pixellate** patch to see this value.

6. Enter 16 as the value and then press the Enter key to see the pixellation double.

7. Select the **Pixellate** patch and press Command-I (⌘-I) to bring up the Inspector.
   Press Command-1 (⌘-1) to show the Input Parameters page of the Inspector if it
   is not already visible.

8. Move the *Scale* slider right and left to see the filter update the image in real time.

Now you know how to route your images through filters and modify their parameters. In the next exercise, you'll reinforce this knowledge by switching out the
Pixellate filter for a **Kaleidoscope**.

Let's try another effect:

1. Go back to the Patch Library, search for the **Kaleidoscope** filter, and drag that
   filter into your composition.

2. Route the image from your **Movie Loader** through the **Kaleidoscope** filter,
   and then out to the **Billboard**, replacing the pixellated image.

3. Select the **Kaleidoscope** patch and press Command-I (⌘-I) to open its Inspector window. Notice that there are many more parameters to play with for the
   Kaleidoscope filter:

   - *Count* and *Angle* can be adjusted with the sliders.

   - *X/Y Centers* can be adjusted by twirling the dials clockwise and
     counterclockwise.

> **Tip**
>
> When using the dials, hold down the Shift key while twirling them to speed up the number changes.

4. Tweak the **Kaleidoscope** settings until you're happy with the output.

Filter Chains and Layering

Follow these steps to see the difference that filter ordering makes:

1. Connect the *Image* output of the **Kaleidoscope** filter to the *Image* input of the **Pixellate** filter, and then connect the **Pixellate** filter's *Image* to the **Billboard**.

   You are now running a simple filter chain. You can create a large variety of effects simply by exploring combinations of various filters.

   Take notice of your output. In this case, your image is running first through the **Kaleidoscope** and then through the **Pixellate** filter, resulting in an output image that is pixellated, but not completely symmetrical, as shown in Figure 3.1.

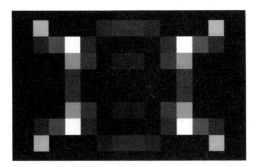

Figure 3.1   The result of a Kaleidoscope > Pixellate filter chain

2. Reroute your *Image* flow so that the image passes first through the **Pixellate** filter and then through the **Kaleidoscope**, ending at the **Billboard**.

   Observe the difference in the output. The squares no longer form a cohesive grid (as shown in Figure 3.2); they are angled to make up the divisions of the **Kaleidoscope**. This chain of effects works especially well with the **Pixellate** *Scale* turned up to approximately 60 and is a great choice for producing an abstract scene from your original movie.

3. Find the **Multiply Blend Mode** patch and drag it into the Editor. Now you will merge the two separate image streams using this compositing patch.

4. Connect the *Image* output of the **Pixellate** patch to the *Image* input on the **Multiply Blend Mode** patch.

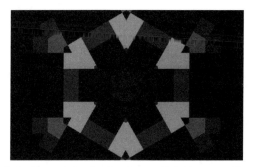

Figure 3.2   The result of a Pixellate > Kaleidoscope filter chain

5. Connect the *Image* output of your **Movie Loader** to the **Kaleidoscope** filter, and then patch the **Kaleidoscope** filter's *Image* output to the *Background Image* input of the **Multiply Blend Mode** patch.

6. Finally, patch the *Image* output of the **Multiply Blend Mode** patch into the **Billboard**.

Now your output displays the result of both filters, using the **Multiply Blend Mode**, as shown in Figure 3.3. This effect should look familiar to you if you've done any compositing with video or imaging programs, such as Adobe Photoshop or Apple Final Cut Pro.

Figure 3.3   The result of combining a pixellated image with a kaleido-scoped copy, using the Multiply Blend mode

Filter Tools

Right now, the two filtered images you've been working with probably are not centered over each other. This arrangement occurs because each layer produces images at a different size, with different *Center* points. To remedy this off-kilter behavior, you can use the Crop filter, which enables you to precisely set the size of your image at any point in the rendering chain.

Image Crop

In the following steps, you'll learn how to use the Image Crop patch to control the rendering size of your images:

1. In the Patch Creator, search for the **Image Crop** patch and drag it into the Editor.

> **Tip**
>
> In Leopard, searching for "crop" will bring up too many patches, because many patches use the word "'crop" in their descriptions. Instead, search for "crops"!

2. Resize the Viewer to 640 × 480 pixels by dragging it from the lower-right corner. The bar at the bottom of the Viewer is updated in real time to let you know the current dimensions of the Viewer.

> **Tip**
>
> You can set the Viewer's aspect ratio by selecting it from the drop-down menu at the lower-left corner of the Viewer. A size of 640 × 480 represents a 4:3 ratio.

3. Route the *Image* output of the **Kaleidoscope** patch through the **Image Crop** patch and then directly to your **Billboard**, as shown in Figure 3.4. Your beautiful output disappears! That's okay. Take a deep breath and forge on.

4. The Viewer is now empty because the **Image Crop** patch creates a 0 × 0 image by default. Open the **Image Crop** patch's Inspector (select the patch and press ⌘-I), and change the *Crop Width* and *Height* to 640 and 480, respectively.

5. The Viewer now displays an output, but it doesn't necessarily look the same as before. You need to set the *Center* of the **Kaleidoscope** patch to put it back in its rightful place. Select the **Kaleidoscope** patch and open its Inspector (⌘-I), and change *Center (X)* and *Center (Y)* to 320 and 240, respectively.

   Now the **Kaleidoscope** is centered. You have set its *Horizontal Center (X)* to be half its width and its *Vertical Center (Y)* to be half its height.

6. Duplicate the **Image Crop** patch and connect the **Pixellate** patch's *Image* output to its *Image* input.

   Before you adjust the settings for this new **Image Crop** patch, you will learn how to tell Quartz Composer to work out some of these math bits automatically.

7. To keep your project organized, double-click the name portion of the **Image Crop** patch attached to your **Kaleidoscope** and type "Kaleidoscope Crop" to rename it, as shown in Figure 3.5. Do the same for the other **Image Crop** patch, renaming it **Pixellate Crop**.

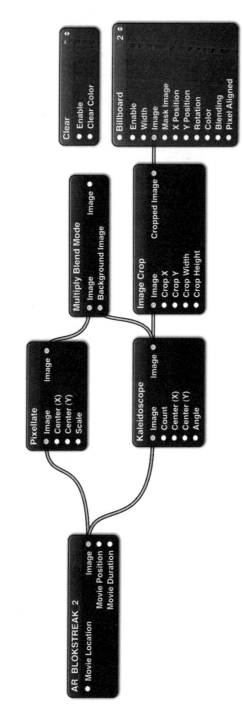

Figure 3.4 The Image data streaming from the Movie Loader to the Kaleidoscope, through the Image Crop, and finally to the Billboard

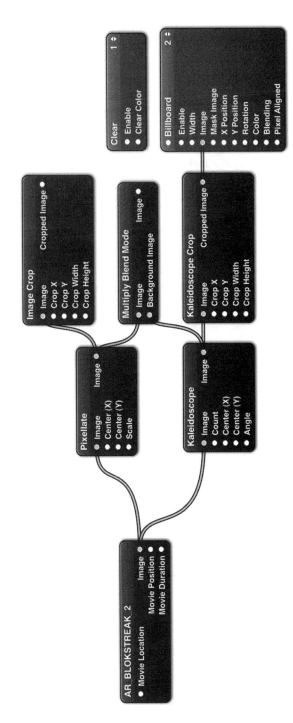

Figure 3.5   The renamed Image Crop patches

27

Rendering Destination Dimensions

To finish the previous exercise, you must learn how to use the **Rendering Destination Dimensions** patch. This patch generates data that you can use to have Quartz Composer automatically resize your image to fit in the Viewer.

1. In the Patch Creator window, find the **Rendering Destination Dimensions** patch and drag it to the Editor.

2. Connect the *Pixels Wide* output of the **Rendering Destination Dimensions** patch to the *Crop Width* of the **Kaleidoscope Crop** patch; next, connect the *Pixels High* output to *Crop Height*.

   You should not see any change, because your rendering destination (i.e., the Viewer) is currently set to 640 × 480 pixels. However, you can now change the size of the Viewer and the image will be adjusted accordingly.

3. Go back to the Patch Creator window, locate the **Math** patch, and add it to the Editor.

4. Connect the *Pixels Wide* output of **Rendering Destination Dimensions** to the **Initial Value** of the **Math** patch—this is the node at the upper-left corner.

5. Use the Inspector (⌘-I) to change *Operation #1* of the **Math** patch to *Divide* and *Operand #1* to *2*.

6. Connect the *Resulting Value* of the **Math** patch (the node in at the upper-right corner) to the *Center (X)* of the **Kaleidoscope** patch.

7. Duplicate the **Math** patch (⌘-D) and drag the new copy off to the side a bit.

> **Tip**
>
> In Leopard, the **Math** patch looks a bit different. It's a full-sized patch like the others, and you can rename it. In this case, you might rename it "Pixels Wide/2" so you can see what it is at a glance.

8. Connect the *Pixels High* output from the **Rendering Destination Dimensions** patch to the *Initial Value* input of the new **Math** patch, and connect its *Resulting Value* to *Center (Y)* on the **Kaleidoscope Crop** patch.

9. To get your pixellated image up to speed, simply connect the *Pixels Wide/High* outputs of the **Rendering Destination Dimensions** patch to the *Crop Width/Height* inputs of the **Pixellate Crop** patch, and connect the two **Math** patch *Resulting Values* to the *Center (X)* and *Center (Y)* inputs on the **Pixellate** patch.

10. Run the cropped image from the **Pixellate Crop** to the *Image* input of the **Multiply Blend Mode** patch. Reconnect the **Multiply Blend Mode** patch's *Output* to the **Billboard**, as shown in Figure 3.6.

Figure 3.6   The final routing, resulting in one image being filtered in two different ways, and then composited upon itself using a Multiply Blend mode

> **Tip**
>
> Snow Leopard provides access to a great library of Virtual Macros assembled by the Quartz Composer team. One of these macros is **Crop To Destination**, which you could use in place of the **Pixellate Crop** and **Kaleidoscope Crop** patches. If you peek inside this macro, you'll see that it's made of a **Rendering Destination Dimensions** patch that feeds its data into an **Image Crop** patch, just like the one you put together.

Whew! Give yourself a pat on the back. That's a lot of patches to deal with simultaneously. You should understand what these patches do and why you need them. If something in this composition doesn't make sense to you, go back through the previous steps, and visually trace the inputs and outputs with your finger. It's important that you become comfortable with the routing logic of Quartz Composer soon.

Core Image FX and FPS

Frames per second (FPS) is a measurement that we use frequently in developing animations. In most cases, you want as high an FPS number as you can get—the more frames your computer can produce every second, the smoother the animation will appear.

Core Image provides image processing technology that utilizes the power of your graphics processor whenever possible. The downside to this approach occurs when your graphics card can't handle the Core Image filter you're trying to use; in that case, your composition and computer will bog down as the operations are routed back to your CPU. Follow these steps to learn about optimizing your compositions and tracking their FPS speed:

1. In the Patch Library, locate the **FPS Display** patch and add it to the Editor. Notice the new visual output that appears at the lower-left corner of the Viewer, as shown in Figure 3.7. The numbers shown here tell you how many frames Quartz Composer is able to fully render every second (Frames Per Second Display).

> **Tip**
>
> When dealing with filters, keep an eye on the FPS and adjust your composition to keep it running smoothly. Ideally, your Quartz composition will run at 60 FPS, which is most likely the limit of your monitor. Keep your compositions running at 20 FPS or higher and you'll be a happy camper.

2. To see the results of an intensive filter, bring in a **Zoom Blur** patch, run the *Image* output from the **Multiply Blend Mode** patch through it, and then route the **Zoom Blur**'s output to the **Billboard**, as shown in Figure 3.8.

3. If you open the **Zoom Blur** patch's Inspector (select the patch and press ⌘-I), you'll notice that the default *Amount* is set to *20*. With this default, you will not

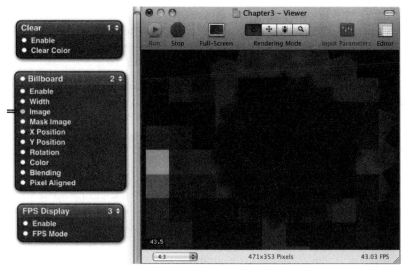

Figure 3.7   The FPS display in the Viewer

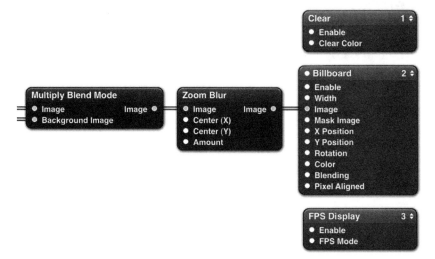

Figure 3.8   Routing the Image through a Zoom Blur patch

see much difference in performance. If you push the *Amount* up much higher, the FPS level will drop. Set the *Amount* too high, and you might slow your whole system down to a crawl. Play around with the *Amount* until you achieve at least 20 FPS.

> **Tip**
>
> If you're using the Quartz Composer in Leopard, you may notice a drop to about 8 FPS even at the default setting of 20. Many Core Image filters perform better under Snow Leopard.

Summary

When working with real-time compositions, it's always a good idea to check the frame rate to see whether the new filter you just added will have a big impact on your FPS. If it does, perhaps you might want to use another filter, or maybe you can lessen the effect to keep your composition running smoothly.

You can also experiment with the Native Core Image Rendering option on the Settings page of your **Billboard** patches. Try turning it on and off, and see which mode gives you better performance—the outcome may be different for each image stream. One rule of thumb: It's better to leave the Native Core Image Rendering option off if you're rendering the image multiple times, as with a picture-in-picture composition.

Challenges

1. Look through the Patch Library for options, and make two more filter chains that you like. Play around with them until they achieve a rate of at least 20 FPS.

2. Try adding different blurs to the chains you just made and note how they change the image. Find the levels for each one at which you can maintain a rate of 20 FPS.

Chapter 4

Using LFOs, Interpolation, and Trackballs to Move Stuff

Chapter 4 already—wow, you are doing well! Okay, so we've given you the lowdown on how to get video working in Quartz Composer (QC) and how to make your movie a bit more interesting with filters. In reality, those steps just scratch the surface of the freedom we have with our 3D world.

This chapter demonstrates some of the cool visual effects that can be created with QC's built-in 3D objects and a couple of nifty "controller" patches that help us develop beautiful organic motion. As with everything in QC, these controller objects can be connected to many different patch parameters, so the techniques you learn here will come in handy for many projects, whether you are trying to rotate cubes, change a color, or generate a numerical range. So pay attention and experiment, experiment, experiment!

 Play the video titled "Interpolation Patch."

This chapter's content makes much more sense if you watch the video with it, so start up this chapter's tutorial now!

Interpolation Patch: Do Stuff for a Bit

The **Interpolation** patch is another example of a complicated word describing something simple, so don't be put off by its fancy name. Instead, have a look and a play with this patch; you'll see it's easy to manipulate. Figure 4.1 shows the **Interpolation** patch.

Figure 4.1   Interpolation patch (Snow Leopard)

Here's how to use the **Interpolation** patch:

1. Launch QC, open a new blank doc, and add a **Clear.**

2. Throw in a **Cube** and change its *Height, Width,* and *Depth* to 0.5. Now look for the **Interpolation** patch in the Patch Creator window. Once you add it to your composition, it will be visible as a controller object (Snow Leopard: black with round edges; Leopard: green with round edges).

3. Make sure your Inspector window is open (⌘-i). It's self-explanatory: Leave the *Start value, End value,* and *Duration* at their defaults, and noodle the *Result* out to the *X pos* of the **Cube** . . . ta-da! You now have a **Cube** that is scrolling center to right once a second, which means it's exactly in time with a 60-bpm hip-hop track, or every other beat of a 120-bpm house track. You see, I told you QC was easy!

Let's explore the other controls of the **Interpolation** patch:

- **Play with the Tension slider and watch the difference:** You can use either a smooth run from the start value to the end, or a kind of a suck or pull effect; the latter is often called easing for those who have done a bit of animation.

- **Change the Repeat mode:** Loop and mirror loop are the choices you will use most often. None and mirror loop once will control stuff if you're focusing on more timed work. Stopping and restarting the composition will allow you to see the effect and avoid the "that didn't do anything" feeling.
- **Interpolation:** This is where a bit of math comes in. Basically, QC gives you even more choices than the Tension slider for controlling how it counts from the start value to the end value. Linear is the normal straight count up; press ⌘-2 (Settings) to see a graph representing the straight-line effect it produces (see Figure 4.2). Change the start value to −1 and the duration to 4 or 8 seconds to make these changes a little clearer.

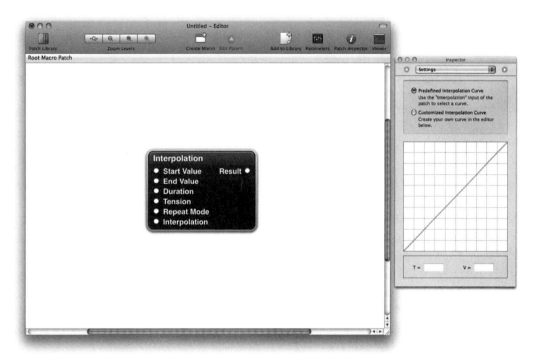

Figure 4.2   The Interpolation patch with its linear interpolation curve
(Snow Leopard)

- **Cycle through the other options—*Quadratic, Cubic, Exponential,* and *Sinusoidal*:** Watch how they affect and smooth the movement between values. These option names are fancy math words for particular shapes of graphs. To check changes to the shape of the graph, press ⌘-2. Pressing ⌘-1 then takes you back to the input parameters so you can make more changes.

If that flexibility isn't enough, QC lets you draw your own graph that it will follow between the start value and the end value! To try this option out while on
the Settings pane (⌘-2), notice the option that appears at the top of the pane:
Predefined curve or Customized curve. Click Customized, and then add points
by clicking the graph and dragging the gradients to make your cube do all kinds
of mad flicks and starts as it travels between the start and end values.

Switch back to predefined interpolation curve so you can learn how to use the
Interpolation patch as an awesome number-crunching utility.

Interpolation as an Amazing Calculator

Suppose you have a cube, which you want to rotate on its Z axis from −84 degrees to
37 degrees. This animation needs to be synced up to some external source—an audio
level, MIDI input, LFO (discussed in the next section), or something else. You could
take the incoming data (which would probably consist of a stream of numbers between
0 and 1) and try to figure out the complicated math on your own, and then pull your
hair out when you decide to change the numbers a little bit and have to do it all over
again—or you can use the **Interpolation** patch to do the math for you.

 Play the video titled "Interpolation as Amazing Calculator."

To solve this problem, follow these steps:

1. Set the *Start Value* of your **Interpolation** to −*84* and the *End Value* to *37*. Set the
   Duration to *1* and the *Repeat Mode* to *None*.

2. Connect the *Result* of the **Interpolation** patch to the *Z Rotation* of the **Cube**.

3. Right-click (or Ctrl-Click) the **Interpolation** patch and choose Timebase >
   External.

4. You now have a *Patch Time* input on your **Interpolation** patch. Insert an **Input
   Splitter** on *Patch Time,* and set its *Minimal and Maximal Values* to *0* and *1,*
   respectively.

5. Click the **Patch Time** input splitter you just created, open its Inspector, and
   look at page 1. Notice the slider labeled "Input." Move this slider left and right,
   and you will see the cube rotating on its Z axis.

You have just abstracted the rotation of this cube, which is an important and powerful technique. The **Patch Time** input splitter that you created could be replaced
with a wide variety of input sources. As long as they provide a stream of numbers
between 0 and 1, your **Interpolation** patch will work to scale them to the proper

range. If your input is between 0 and 100 instead, there's no problem: Just set the *Duration* of the **Interpolation** patch to 100, and you're in business. The idea here is that instead of referring to the system clock to obtain its current time, the **Interpolation** patch can look to any input that generates numbers for this value.

Play around with this setup and keep the underlying idea in the back of your head. Although this technique may seem strange now, there will come a time when you need to transform a stream of numbers, and you can revisit this exercise for a refresher course. (You will also reuse this technique in upcoming tutorials in this book.)

LFO

If you liked the smooth moves of the fancier waves in the **Interpolation** patch, or if you want to create some really smooth, gentle organic motion, you will want to master the **LFO** controller (see Figure 4.3). Does LFO mean "little fun object"? Not quite. It actually stands for "low-frequency oscillator." If you are into music production, you have probably come across these kinds of devices; if not, don't worry. Using LFO is easy once you know how.

Figure 4.3   LFO patch (Snow Leopard)

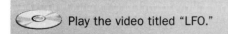 Play the video titled "LFO."

Keep working from the open composition:

1. Reset the **Interpolation** to a predefined curve, with *Start:* 0; *End:* 1; *Duration:* 1; *Repeat Mode:* loop; and *Interpolation:* linear. Also change the **Cube**'s *Y Position* to 0.5.

2. Duplicate the **Cube** (⌘-d) and change its *Y Position* to −0.5.

3. Use the Patch Creator to add an **LFO** patch to your composition.

4. There are not so many obvious labels on this patch, but recall that the sinusoidal option in the **Interpolation** essentially represented a sine wave—a lovely smooth wave that runs from −1 to 1. The **LFO** patch gives you fine control over such a wave, so let's connect it up and see what happens. Noodle the *Result* to the *Y Position* of your second lower **Cube** . . . ta smooth da.

5. Let's break down what we did. In the Inspector window (⌘-i), you can experiment with the controls:

   ▪ **Type:** The kind of wave you have. The sin and cos options are pretty sweet swingers; triangle and square not so much. Sawtooth can be fun, random is always interesting, and PWM relates to the setting of the same name further down the list. Figure 4.4 provides a few images of the waves that should help you understand how they will behave. As always, you should experiment with them all to see which ones you like.

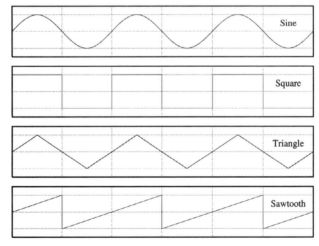

Figure 4.4   Waveforms

- **Period:** How long a wave cycle takes. It is quite similar to the duration of the interpolation.

- **Phase:** The point at which the cycle starts. A range of 0–360 allows you to offset the wave on the X axis, which is useful if you have a lot of sin waves and want them to behave differently within the same value limits.

- **Amplitude:** How big the wave will be. From start to end, the range of values is $X2$, as the waves go in both positive and negative directions. Thus entering 360 for a rotation will actually give you 720 degrees of spin as the wave will swing from −360 to +360.

- **Offset:** Assuming a value 0, the offset allows you to push or pull the wave by moving it on the Y axis. Thus, if you want a 0 to 360-degree rotation, you would set the amplitude to 180 and the offset to 180; then a wave that would have occurred over the −180 to +180 range is pushed up 180 amp in the positive direction (see Figure 4.5).

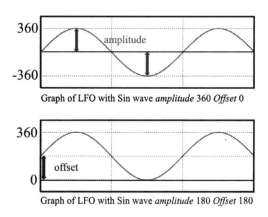

Graph of LFO with Sin wave *amplitude* 360 *Offset* 0

Graph of LFO with Sin wave *amplitude* 180 *Offset* 180

Figure 4.5   A 180-amp wave before and after offset

- **PWM Ratio:** You can probably survive your whole QC life without touching this wave, but for those who must know about it, search for my ninja research.

6. Save the file at this stage as `controllers.qtz` or similar.

Hierarchies with Environment Patches: Trackball and 3D Transformation

Once you start experimenting with the **Interpolation** and **LFO** patches, you will quickly run into the "Where the heck did that cube go?" phenomenon. Recall that the Viewer is like a camera pointed in a 3D world: It "sees" only from about −2 to 2 on the X axis and from −1.5 to 1.5 on the Y axis. As a consequence, if you move any object's positioning values outside that range, the object will disappear offscreen. This can be effective when you mean for this behavior to occur, but it can be frustrating when you don't. But have no fear—hope is at hand. A couple of special patches allow us to control where the Viewer points. To use these patches, we first need to discuss a new category of patches: Environment patches.

Environment patches bring us to another key difference between QC and programs you may have used in the past for creating movies. QC allows things to be put inside stuff, so that you can create hierarchies as well as connect patches together. For example, we can put some patches inside another patch, and then other patches inside that. In turn, each time you go inside an Environment patch, you have a whole blank Editor in which to start patching within it. The best way to think of this approach is by seeing it as analogous to groups in your layers of Photoshop, or parenting in Aftereffects; any patches you place "inside" an Environment patch will be affected by it.

Let's get back to the problem at hand—cubes (and such) moving out of the Viewer's "sight." The **Trackball** and **3D Transformation** Environment patches act almost like a 3D camera, in which we can control the position, rotation, and zooming of the patches within them as seen by the Viewer. First, let's explore the **Trackball** patch, which allows us to click and drag on the Viewer window to rotate objects, a bit like a 3D modeling programs interface.

 Play the video titled "Trackball and 3D Transformation."

Trackball

One of the most natural steps you want to take to find stuff that has "disappeared" is move the camera to look for it. That's exactly what the **Trackball** allows you to do— to click on the Viewer window and move stuff around the screen. How you achieve that goal is by putting stuff you want to be able to move around in this way "inside" the **Trackball**. That might sound a little confusing, but it's grand.

Let's continue working with the same composition we made earlier this chapter:

1. Add a **Trackball** patch from the Patch Creator/Patch Library window.

2. Click and drag on the Editor to select your two **Cubes** and controllers, and then cut them from the display (⌘-x).

3. Double-click the **Trackball** object to enter it (make sure CAPS LOCK is off or this technique won't work), and paste the **Cubes** and controllers there (⌘-v).

4. Click the Viewer and drag the mouse to move around the view. Amazing!

While this approach is great for looking for lost stuff and allowing you to create some cool new angles on your cubes, it is just used for looking around in your current session. When you save your composition—which, of course, you are doing regularly (right?)— unfortunately, Quartz Composer doesn't remember which way you left the **Trackball**.

Try it now:

1. Save your composition as `Trackball and controllers.qtz`.
2. Close both the Editor and the Viewer (⌘-w-x2).
3. Open the composition again (File > Open Recent). The **Trackball** patch will be reset to its standard view.

But suppose you want to stop that reversion to the standard view from happening. How can you keep your cool side view of the cubes? **3D Transformation** has it under control.

3D Transformation

Like the **Trackball** patch, **3D Transformation** is an Environment patch, so you will have to double-click it and either paste in objects or add new ones from the Patch Creator/Patch Library. Like the **Trackball**, your objects can then be manipulated in 3D space, but not by clicking and dragging with the mouse; instead, you change the parameters of the patch to work with them.

Working with the `controllers.qtz` composition:

1. Add a **3D Transformation** patch from the Patch Creator/Patch Library window.
2. Click and drag the Editor to select your two **Cubes** and controllers, and then cut them from the display (⌘-x).
3. Double-click the **3D Transformation** object to enter it (make sure CAPS LOCK is off or this technique won't work), and paste the **Cubes** and controllers there (⌘-v).
4. Open the Inspector window (⌘-i) and try the *Enable:* On/Off switch.

   Now we'll work through all the other options:

   - *Rotation Origin X, Y, Z:* The same as the "anchor point" you probably have come across in Photoshop, Illustrator, Motion, Aftereffects, or their ilk. If these values are left at 0 0 0, the objects in the **3D Transformation** object will be rotated about the middle (a good choice for simple rotations). Alternatively, you can offset the rotation a bit if you want something to spin on its corner rather than its midpoint, for example. If you are like me, you will rarely use these three values, because the next six are the real deal.

   - *Rotation X, Y, Z:* Just like the **Cube**'s own *X, Y, Z Rotation* but affect all patches inside the **3D Transformation**. To recap, these values specify how much you want to spin the object and in which direction. The range is 0 to 360 in degrees. If you are more comfortable working with percentages, think of it this way: 360 = 100% rotation. To help you remember which one to change, *X* is front flips, *Y* is spin on your toes, and *Z* is fall over sideways.

   - *Translation X, Y, Z:* Like the *XYZ Positions* of the **Cube**, **Sprite**, and other objects, but again affect all the elements within the **3D Transformation**.

Thus, if your **Cube** is on 0,4 *X* positioning and inside a **3D Transformation** that has 1.8 *X* positioning, it will not be visible. However, if you set the *Z* value of the **3D Transformation** to −2, then you will be able to see it again as the *Z* plane effectively zooms the view in and out . . . Get it? No? Try setting this up in a composition and experimenting until you understand what is happening.

5. Now it's time to bring everything together. **Trackball** is great for quickly looking at what you are doing, and **3D Transformation** is great for actually moving things around. In my own work, I normally use both. Let's add a **Trackball** to the composition.

6. Select and cut the **3D Transformation**.

7. Double-click the **Trackball** patch to enter inside it.

8. Paste the **3D Transformation** inside the **Trackball** patch. Now you have two layers of hierarchy, and you can click and drag to quickly see "what's going on" with your objects as well as change **3D Transformation** settings so any cool views you make will be persistent.

9. Start experimenting with connecting controllers to the **3D Transformation** and then inside that patch to the **Cube**. This is where the fun really starts!

Tip

Always click Reset for any **Trackballs** present in your patch before changing **3D Transformation** values. Both affect how you see objects in the Viewer.

Summary

We covered a lot of ground in this chapter, so watch all of the videos a few times to make sure you understand everything. Here are some key points to remember:

- We can control objects using the **Interpolation** and **LFO** patches, making them move or rotate very smoothly or to a beat.

- In QC, some patches allow us to place other patches within them. For example, the **Trackball** patch acts like a camera, in which we can move any objects inside it with the mouse. The **3D Transformation** patch also allows us to zoom and spin objects, but it is controlled only from the patches parameters.

Challenges

You now have some powerful controller objects at your disposal. The challenge for this chapter is to create a simple scene with a number of different objects moving around it, and then to use a 3D transformation to spin them all around as if a camera were orbiting around the scene.

Chapter 5

Debugging (When Things Go Wrong)

With the power of experimentation in Quartz Composer come the inevitable "What did I do wrong?" moments. Here are some helpful patches to get users through these tough times.

 Play the video titled "Make and Use Debugging Tools."

Using Image with String

You will learn about the official debugging tools available for Quartz Composer in the next section. For now, let's construct a handy on-screen debug display by learning how to print text to a **Billboard**:

1. Create a new composition and place a **Clear** patch and an **Image with String** patch into the editor.

2. Insert a **Billboard** patch and route the **Image with String**'s *Image* output to the **Billboard**.

3. Connect the *Display Width* output of the **Image with String** patch to the **Billboard**'s *Width* input, and set the **Billboard**'s *Blending* to *Over*.

4. Set the *Font Size* of the **Image with String** patch to *0.25*, and the *Horizontal Alignment* to *Left*.

You have now created a handy on-screen debugger that looks something like Figure 5.1. If something is not working correctly, you can route data to the *String* input and see it appear in your output window, even in full-screen mode. Next, you'll turn

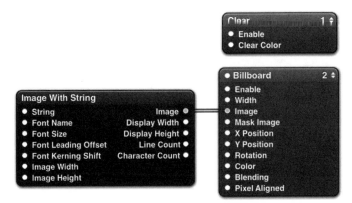

Figure 5.1   The classic "Hello World" setup

this patch combination into a Virtual Macro that you can easily reuse, similar to the way it is used in Figure 5.2.

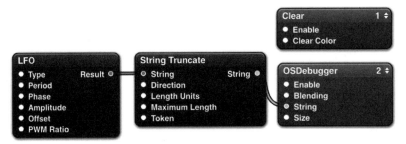

Figure 5.2   Printing an LFO patch's input to the Viewer in a readable fashion

1. Right-click (or Control-Click) on the **Image with String** patch, and choose Publish Inputs > String. Press Enter to confirm the default key "String" as the input name.

2. Right-click on the **Billboard** and choose Publish Inputs > Blending so that you can access the blend later.

3. Insert an **Input Splitter** for the *Font Size* of the **Image with String** patch by right-clicking on it and choosing Insert Input Splitter > Font Size.

4. In the Inspector for this new **Input Splitter**, set its *Minimal Value* to *0.05* and its *Maximal Value* to *0.75*. These choices create a handy slider that you can use later to resize your debugger display.

5. Publish the input of this **Input Splitter** as *Size*.

6. Draw a box around the **Image with String** and **Billboard** patches to select them, and choose Editor > Add to Library from the Quartz Composer toolbar. Name your new Virtual Macro "OSDebugger," and fill in whatever you like for the *Copyright* and *Description*.

> **Tip**
>
> To create a new Clip in Leopard, select your patches and click the Create Clip icon at the top of the Quartz Composer Editor.

7. Look in your Patch Library; you should now see a patch called **OSDebugger** that will accept a string input and print it directly to the screen.

8. Bring an **LFO** patch into the Editor, and route its *Result* to the *String* input of the **OSDebugger**.

   With the default settings, you'll see a value that oscillates between 0 and 0.9, which is a very long value.

9. To simplify this number, add a **Round** patch to the Editor, and route the **LFO**'s *Result* first through it, and then on to the **OSDebugger**. Your output will now switch between 0 and 1—a little too simplified.

10. Add a **String Truncate** patch in place of your **Round** patch, routing the **LFO**'s *Result* through the *String* input. Your number will, by default, truncate to nine digits (plus the "." separator). Use the Inspector on your **String Truncate** patch to trim the output to three digits (remember, that's four characters), and remove the "..." token.

11. Now your output is reasonably readable, though it's still running at light speed. Play with the settings on the **LFO** patch to change the on-screen display. (Hint: Start by changing the period to a larger value, such as 50, to slow things down.)

Debugging Tips

Take your Viewer out of full-screen mode if you have it running that way (by giving the Viewer focus and clicking Esc; see Figure 5.3). Notice the Rendering Mode options that appear at the top of the Viewer, in the center. By default, you should be running in Performance mode. There are three more modes to try: Debug, Interactive, and Profile.

Figure 5.3   The composition rendering modes

> **Tip**
>
> In Leopard, only three Rendering Mode buttons are available; the Interactive Placement mode was introduced in Snow Leopard.

Interactive Placement Mode

In Interactive Placement mode, objects such as sprites and billboards can be moved around by dragging-and-dropping them with your mouse directly in the Viewer.

Debug Mode

Switching to Debug mode opens a drawer from the bottom of the Viewer, where errors will be output if and when they occur. You can also push data to this drawer by using the **Log** patch. You will need to enable private patches to gain access to this tool. Additionally, your Editor will become quite flashy.

Each patch will flash red when it's executing, and your Viewer will show red wherever it is updating the screen.

> **Tip**
>
> At the time of this book's writing, Debug mode had the unhappy habit of freezing the user interface if the composition is complex (lots of iterations and other features); be judicious when using Debug mode, and minimize your iterations, copies, and particles if possible.

Debug Mode in Leopard

In Leopard, three colors are used to indicate what is going on in Debug mode:

- Green shading indicates that the patch is enabled and running.
- Red shading indicates that the patch is not enabled and does not affect the composition.
- Orange indicates that a patch is enabled but not running; it will turn green when processing data.

Profile Mode

Switching to Profile mode opens a drawer from the right-hand side of the Viewer, with real-time graphs profiling your patch. This is a good place to look when your patch has slowed down and you're trying to figure out why.

Summary

In this chapter, you learned different ways to inspect what is going on in your composition to help you figure out why something isn't working, or to improve overall performance. Quartz Composer gives you great power to debug while your composition is running, so make sure to use its debugging tools as you create and explore the application.

Challenges

Open up the composition you made in Chapter 3 and switch to Debug mode to see what's going on under the hood. Reroute signal flows to see how they change the debugging output.

Chapter 6

Particles (Little Flying Bits of Bling)

By this stage, you have some sweet patches and are beginning to feel as if you might have a clue about how to ninja up something awesome with Quartz Composer (QC). At the same time, perhaps things are feeling a little blocky when you were hoping for some subtlety and beauty—a tool to make the pixels dance. Well, this is the chapter for you! Here we crack open a new can of whoop ass that I like to call particles. Funnily enough, that's what QC calls this feature, too.

The **Particle System** in QC is quite versatile. Aside from creating elements, which are beautiful in their own right, we can use the **Particle System** to "model" or recreate complex real-world events, such as rain, water, and even explosions!

As we dance our merry particle dance, we will also come across blend modes. "Blend" is a fancy term that describes how things look when they overlap. For you Photoshoppers out there, this will be familiar territory. For newbies, don't worry: These capabilities just give us yet more options to experiment with!

Before we jump into this part of the lesson, let's make a Clip to speed up your development.

Video tutorial on!

 Play the video titled "Adding Your Patches to the Library."

Add to Library (Creating a Clip in Leopard)

Developing with QC can sometimes feel like you do the same thing over and over, which is kind of what computers are good at. There must be a better way, right? Right.

As you discovered in Chapter 5 when you created your **OSDebugger**, the Add to Library feature allows you to add a chunk of patches or compositions that you use often to your Patch Library. You can also exchange these patches with your friends by adding them to the following locations (where USERFOLDER is your home folder):

USERFOLDER/Library/Graphics/Quartz Composer Patches (Snow Leopard)

USERFOLDER/Library/Application Support/Apple/Developer Tools/ Quartz Composer/Clips (Leopard)

These chunks added to your Patch Library are technically called Virtual Macros. The good thing is that even after you add Virtual Macros to a composition, you can still edit them. To edit one, click on the Virtual Micro in Patch Library to select it, Control-click the patch name, and select Edit Virtual Macro. Once you make and save your changes, all opened compositions that use the Virtual Macro will be automatically updated.

We created some useful chunks to go with this book, which you can find in the Goodies folder on the DVD. You are free to use the macros provided; however, to be a true QC ninja, you need to know how to make your own. Here, we show you how to create an **LFO** patch preset for a rotation. Recall that when you add an **LFO** from the Patch Library, its default range is 0 to 1; for rotation, however, we want a range of 0 to 360.

Here's how to make the "LFO for Rotation" Virtual Macro:

1. Add an **LFO** patch from the Patch Library.

2. Use the Patch Inspector (⌘-i if it is not already open) to set the *Amplitude* and *Offset* to 180 and the *Period* to 30.

3. Right-Control-click on the **LFO** in the Editor, select Publish Input > Period, enter the rotation duration, and then press Enter to confirm the change.

4. Right-Control-click on the **LFO** patch in the Editor, select Publish Output > Result, and name it "rotation output."

5. Click on the **LFO** patch in the Editor to make sure it is selected, and then click the Add to Library button on the top of the interface (Leopard: Create Clip).

6. A window pops up in which you can add some details for your Virtual Macro. This information will be used in the Patch Library, so fill the details in so you can find them later. Name: "LFO for rotation"; Copyright: (your name!); Description: "LFO with amp and offset to 180 period published."

7. Now, here comes the fun bit. Open a new blank composition (⌘-Shift-n).

8. In the Patch Library search bar, start typing "LFO for rotation"—and there it is! Add it to the composition—and there it is! Try adding a **Cube** or **Sprite** and connecting up your new patch to see how it works.

Starting Point Composition

Now you have seen how simple this process is, you can create your own little library of patches. In addition to being able to create parts of patches, we want you to consider your starting point for your compositions. It can be really tedious to add the same patches every time you want to start something new. To streamline this process, we'll create a basic starting point composition furnished with the usual suspects—**Clear, Trackball,** and **3D Transformation.**

 Play the video titled "Creating Your Starting Point Composition."

Here's how to make the starting point composition:

1. Launch QC and select File > New blank (⌘-Shift-n).
2. Add a Clear: Patch Creator (⌘-Alt) > **Clear.**
3. For maximum 3D working, add a **3D Transformation.**
4. Double-click to enter the **3D Transformation** patch, and then add a **Trackball** there.
5. Double-click to enter the Trackball patch, and then add a **Sprite.** This is where we want to start from for each new composition.
6. Save this composition to your desktop so you have a handy starting point for the rest of the book's lessons.

The Particle System

Now that we have those little time savers sorted out, let's get down to the **Particle System** (see Figure 6.1):

 Play the video titled "The Particle System."

1. Use the Patch Library/Patch Creator to find **Particle System.** After clicking through the patches, add it to the bottom level of your blank composition, where the **Sprite** is located.
2. Delete the **Sprite** (click it and press Del), leaving behind just the **Particle System.**

Figure 6.1   Particle System patch

As we can see from the lighter shade and the rounded corners, **Particle System** is a render-type patch. We might expect to see something in the Viewer immediately—and, sure enough, there are a bunch of white squares grooving away.

Before we get into the details, it's a good idea to understand what a "particle system" is. The word *system* suggests, and what you see on screen is, more than just one thing; that is, a system includes many items that play off one another. In essence, a particle system is a bit like a shower, where the emitter is like the showerhead and the particles are like the millions of little water droplets shooting out of the showerhead. In turn, the particle system gives you absolute control of the shower room, much as in a shower you can control how fast the water comes out (minimum and maximum velocities). In the virtual world, of course, you can also change stuff you can't alter in the real world. For example, water always runs downhill under earth's gravity, but in a particle system you can flip that behavior around so that the water flows up toward the ceiling (enter a negative value for gravity) or you can make a video play on every drop of water (attach a video to the image input).

Particle System is an incredibly flexible patch. I return to it again and again, change a few settings, and get something totally new—so experiment, experiment, experiment!

The **Particle System** patch has a rather large number of parameters, some of which affect the emitter (showerhead) and some of which affect the rest of the system (how the water looks or flows out of the showerhead). Don't be too worried—some of these items will look very familiar. For example, the *X, Y,* and *Z Positions* are just the same as for **Cubes** and **Sprites**, but in this case they control the emitter location. The *Color* and *Image* settings are also the same as for the other patches, but here affect the particles.

Let's explore the other parameters:

- *Particle Count:* You guessed it—this parameter counts the particles! Its behavior depends on your particle effect. If you are running videos on each of your particles, for example, this can stress your computer out. If everything starts to slow down at any point, try reducing this number; consider it the first place to try to fix the application.

- *X, Y, Z Min* and *Max Velocity:* Velocity = the speed of the particle; *X, Y, Z* = the direction in which the particle is going. Particles will move at various speeds ranging from the minimum to the maximum value. You can use this setting to point the showerhead where you want it and to spray particles everywhere or just in a narrow line. Change the *X Min* from −1 to 0 to see what I mean.

- *Min* and *Max Size:* Rather than just having one setting for size, to keep things looking more natural you can set the particle system to spray particles out in varying sizes between these two values. Of course, if you make both the *Min* and *Max* values the same, then all particles will be the same size—but that makes it all a little boring.

- *Lifetime:* Select the color setting and the color wheel part, and then slowly drag the mouse, gradually changing the color of the particles. Notice that the particles take a wee second to get from the emitter to the outside of the system. Just as the shower water runs down the drain, the particles disappear after a while. The *Lifetime* setting controls how long any individual particle will be visible, from starting at the emitter to flowing out of the system. The slightly complex part of this operation occurs when you have set a big size and velocity and you shorten the *Lifetime*; then the particles have less time to grow to their maximum size and reach their maximum velocity. In essence, changing this setting has the effect of speeding up the flow of particles. As this example demonstrates, the different settings are interconnected—and that's why getting particles to do what you want can take a bit of practice!

- *Attraction:* Bit of a weird one. This setting determines how much the particles want to be near the emitter. If you give *Attraction* a value of 2, for example, the particles fly out and are then sucked back into the emitter. In contrast, if the value is set too high, the particles go nuts. Obviously, this setting affects the overall flow of the particles, just like their sizes, velocities, and lifetimes.

- *Gravity:* Just like the thing that keeps us stuck to planet earth. The larger the number, the more the particles are pulled downward. Conversely, with a negative value for *Gravity*, the particles fly off to the ceiling. Of course, if you rotated the *X* rotation of the **3D Transformation** patch, gravity will also control how much the particles fly at you or away from you—but let's not get too complex yet.

- *Blending:* This setting is covered in the following section. For now, try all three options and you'll get the idea of how it works.

- *Size Delta:* Over the lifetime of each particle, its size changes from when it leaves the emitter to when it disappears or "dies"; the *Size Delta* setting determines just how much it changes. With a positive value, the particle size grows and grows; with a negative value, it shrinks. A value of −1 will create an interesting flicker effect. These effects must also be balanced against the other settings at work on the particle's motion.

- *Red, Green, Blue, Opacity, Delta*: These settings control how the color and opacity of the particles change over their lifetime. If you want the particles to fade away to black as they travel from the emitter to the edge of your system, enter a negative value in the opacity delta; if you want them to brighten up, add a positive value. Try changing the color setting to red; the R, G, and B deltas to 0; opacity to −1; and gravity to −1. You can see the beginnings of a fire-type effect with these choices, which leads us on to the next section—real-world modeling.

Real-World Modeling

As we saw at the end of the settings description, a little mucking around can create some interesting models or replications of real-world events. Once you have experimented enough with the **Particle System** to have a basic grasp of its settings, consider the real-world situation you are trying to model and then work backward from that.

Rain

Rain falls down; its drops are small and wet. Additionally, consider the final product before deciding how to model rain. Rain has been represented in film, comics, and animation in a variety of ways, so your audience should be able to recognize it fairly easily. Is one of those styles more suitable? Another good way to approach modeling is to consider real-world fakes. For example, to create rain for a scene in cinema, filmmakers use a trough-type thing that is placed above the camera view and has many small holes through which liquid falls.

Have a go yourself and then watch what I did. Does your attempt look better? Send it to us!

Play the video titled "Making Rain."

Follow these steps to recreate the `rain.qtz` file in the resource folder:

1. Add a new **Particle System** in the starting point Clip.

2. Rain falls from the top. I moved the emitter *Y Position* up to just off screen to mimic this behavior.

3. For the system's *Image,* I chose a very simple teardrop gradient. You are free to use your own image. Add your own image or `rain_particle.jpg` from the resource folder to your composition.

4. Connect the **rain_particle**'s *Image* output to **Particle System**'s *Image* input.

5. Change **Particle System**'s *Blend mode* to *Addition.*

6. The output looks okay, but it's spraying too wide. Limit the *X Min* and *Max* to *0.3.*

7. Now the whole rain effect looks very narrow and dense—not really what we're after. Let's decrease the *Particle Count.*

8. Duplicate the **Particle System** four times, reattaching the same **rain_particle** *Image* output to each copy.

9. Set various *X positions* to space them out.

10. Now we are getting somewhere. Rain doesn't often fall in sheets, so to add more interest, I throw in four **LFO** patches to slowly move each of the four rain systems a bit on the *X* axis.

11. Change the *Period* and *Phase* settings so the motion of each system doesn't look too similar to the motion of the other systems.

12. Experiment with each system until you're happy with the final look. It's not the most convincing rain shower in the world, but for 5 minutes' work it's not bad. Further work could be to add a photo of a dark sky on a **Sprite** in the background, add more systems, and so on.

Fire

At the end of the section "The Particle System," we were on our way to creating a fire-type look. See if you can work out how to finesse it.

 Play the video titled "Making Fire."

Here's my method:

1. Add a **Particle System**.
2. Change *Gravity* to −2.
3. Change the *RGB Deltas* to *0* and the *Opacity Delta* to −1.
4. The next step is to get an appropriate particle image. If you watch a fire burn, what does it consist of? Lots of little flames! I grabbed a flame image (see Figure 6.2) and added that, but it looks a bit square and nasty. To fix it, I try decreasing the *Min* and *Max Size* values.

Figure 6.2   Flame image

5. I change the *Blend mode* to *Add* but am still not happy.
6. Let's grab the stock image and bring it into an image editing program; we'll put a radial gradient fade to black around the whole flame image (see Figure 6.3).

Figure 6.3   Flame image with radial gradient fade applied

7. When we bring this image back into the composition, it looks hot!
8. Limit the range of motion to make the flame look more realistic. That should be enough to represent fire to your audience.
9. To make it even better, try using three **Particle Systems** overlaying one another, with variations on the flame image, as real fire never repeats itself.

> **Tip**
> OpenCL allows you to have full control over **Particle Systems**. For more information, check `http://developer.apple.com/library/mac/#samplecode/OpenCL/Introduction/Intro.html#//apple_ref/doc/uid/DTS40009236`.

Blend Modes

Blend modes control how images and video interact when they overlay each other or get in the way of each other as you look at them in the Viewer. Sometimes, we want to see only the front-most object (e.g., when trying to model solid objects). At other times, we want to be able to see through objects (e.g., when modeling fire or rain).

The basic Blend modes of *Add, Replace,* and *Overlay* are available in most of the basic shape and object patches within QC. Photoshop users will be familiar with a range of blending options, but don't worry—these can all be achieved through the "composite" patches. If you type "blend" into the Patch Creator, you will see many patches of this type; they take two image inputs and give one mixed output.

As with everything in QC, it's all about experimentation. To start your own exploration, try working with Steamshift's **Blendmode Explorer** patch, which is included in the Resource folder on the book's DVD.

Summary

In this chapter, you learned how to make Clips so you can create shortcuts for parts of compositions that you'll find yourself making over and over again. We also discovered the **Particle System**, a patch that allows us to model flows of small objects rather than single static objects. The subtle interaction of many of its parameters means that the more time you spend experimenting with this bad boy, the cooler and more interesting the stuff you can make! Finally, we explored Blend modes to find creative ways of compositing two stills or movies.

Challenges

Experiment with adding more patches to your Virtual Macros, and build up your own library of handy tools. Also try modeling your own real-world example using a **Particle System**.

Chapter 7

Mouse Input (Making Your Mouse Do Cool Stuff)

The mouse is an excellent input device for interactive work, and most computers will have one. This tutorial will use a three-button mouse as the example device, although you can use a single-button mouse or the trackpad on your laptop instead.

 Play the video titled "Introduction to Particles."

Particle Systems Control

The first thing you'll do is create a simple **Particle System** that reacts to the mouse:

1. Create a new composition, and add a **Clear** patch and a **Particle System** patch.

2. Add an **Image with String** patch, and connect its *Image* output to the *Image* input of the **Particle System**.

3. Set the *String* of the **Image with String** patch to " •" (that's two spaces and then a bullet; option 8).

4. Set the **Particle System**'s properties as follows:

   X Min Velocity: 0.1

   X Max Velocity: 0.1

   Y Min Velocity: −0.1

   Y Max Velocity: 0.1

   Z Min Velocity: −0.1

   Z Max Velocity: 0.1

   Attraction: 0

   Blend: Add

You've now created a **Particle System** (Figure 7.1), which is nothing new; you had plenty of practice with that in Chapter 6. Up next is the fun part—adding in mouse control.

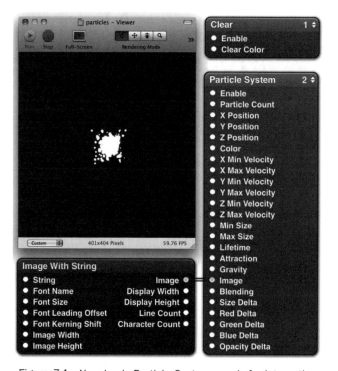

Figure 7.1   Your basic Particle System, ready for interaction

5. Add a **Mouse** patch to the Editor, and connect its X and Y *Position* outputs to the X and Y *Position* inputs of the **Particle System** patch.

   The results are immediately enjoyable. Move your mouse over the Viewer, and the particles now erupt from your pointer. To make the composition more interactive, you'll modify this setup so that a mouse click starts and stops the drawing of the particles.

   This goal could be accomplished by controlling the *Enable* input of the **Particle System**, but the result would be a very abrupt start and stop: The particles would all disappear immediately, and a cloud of them would then reappear when you pressed the mouse button again. Instead, we'll modify the *Color* setting of the **Particle System**, bringing the particles' *Alpha* level up and down.

6. Add an **HSL Color** patch to your composition. Connect the *Color* output to the *Color* input of the **Particle System**.

7. Decrease the *Luminosity* of the **HSL Color** patch to *0.5*, which will allow color to show through. Change the *Hue* to switch the color, if you'd like.

8. Connect the *Left Button* output from the **Mouse** patch to the *Alpha* input of the **HSL Color** patch.

Now when you click your mouse in the Viewer, particles begin erupting, and they stop when you let go. Really, the particles still exist, but because you've set their *Alpha* value to 0, they are invisible. Your composition should look similar to Figure 7.2.

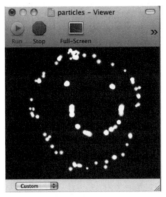

Figure 7.2   To draw this smiley face, set the Start-Up Delay and Particle Lifetime to 6; the X, Y, and Z Velocities to a Min of −0.01 and a Max of 0.01; and the Attraction to 0.

Smoothing Input

Let's turn our **Particle System** into more of a comet that will chase the cursor. We will accomplish this by adding **Smooth** patches and experimenting with their interpolations.

1. Set the following properties for the **Particle System** (see Figure 7.3):

   Particle Count: 500 (less if this drags your system down)

   X Min Velocity: −0.25

   X Max Velocity: 0.25

   Y Min Velocity: −0.25

   Y Max Velocity: 0.25

   Z Min Velocity: 0

   Z Max Velocity: 0

   Min Size: .1

   Max Size: 0.15

Lifetime: 2

Attraction: 0

Gravity: 1

Blending: Add

Size Delta: −0.05

Red through *Opacity Delta*s: 0

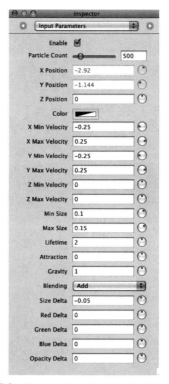

Figure 7.3   New settings for the Particle System

2. Bring two **Smooth** patches into your composition, and route your **Mouse**'s *X* and *Y Position* data through them, individually, as shown in Figure 7.4.

   Now the comet chases your cursor, lagging behind until you stop and wait for it to catch up. These **Smooth** patches are a must for noisy inputs like accelerometers, and they can be helpful in slowing down and smoothing out animations anywhere you have input streams, especially if they are human generated.

3. There are a few controllable parameters for your **Smooth** patches. Change the *Increasing Duration* for your *X Position* data to *0.1*, leaving the *Decreasing Duration* at *1.0*.

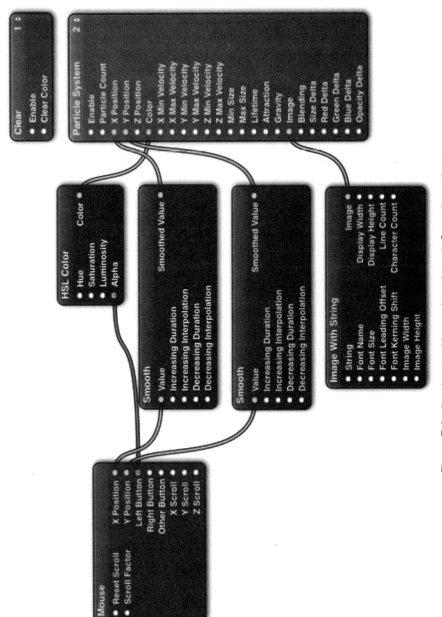

Figure 7.4 Routing the Mouse data through Smooth patches

Now move your comet around. Notice how the comet follows your cursor very closely when you move from left to right across the Viewer (in an increasing fashion), but still drags behind the cursor when you move it the opposite way.

4. Reset the *Increasing Duration* to *1.0*, and change all of the *Interpolations* to *Exponential In*. There are four in total—two for each **Smooth** patch.

Now the comet makes a slow start toward your cursor, but then moves exponentially faster as it nears the cursor. You can use this behavior to play a game of tag with the comet, moving your cursor away from it at the last moment.

5. Switch the *Interpolations* to *Exponential Out* to experience the difference.

The comet will follow the cursor much faster, coming to a smooth stop as it nears the cursor. *Exponential In-Out* will combine the two patterns: The comet will take its time ramping up speed toward your cursor, and then come in for a smooth landing once it reaches that point.

Try out combinations of different interpolation styles and durations to see which sorts of movements you can create. Make sure to save this composition, as you'll be using it again in a later chapter!

 Play the video titled "How to Use the Interaction Patches."

Drag-and-Drop Interaction

The ability to drag and drop **Billboard** and **Sprite** patches is new in Quartz Composer for Snow Leopard. This exercise will show you how simple it is to set up multiple drag-and-drop items and apply physics effects to them.

1. Start a new composition, and add a **Clear** patch and a **Sprite** patch.

2. Add an **Interaction** patch to the Editor.

Notice that the **Interaction** patch has a connection point on the same line as the header—just above *Mouse Down*. This *interaction port* specifies which consumer patch it will control.

3. Connect the *interaction port* of the **Interaction** patch to the *interaction port* of the **Sprite** patch, which appears immediately to the left of the header label "Sprite," as shown in Figure 7.5.

4. Connect the *X* and *Y Position* outputs of the **Interaction** patch to the *X* and *Y Position* inputs of the **Sprite**, and set the **Sprite**'s *Width* and *Height* to *0.25*.

Now you can drag and drop the sprite to any portion of the screen, directly in the Viewer.

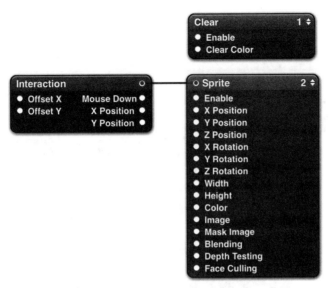

Figure 7.5   Connecting the Interaction patch to the Sprite for interactive control

5. To create another interactive object, select the **Interaction** and **Sprite** patches, and press ⌘-D to duplicate them.

   Now you've got two moveable sprites with very exact movement. To add a little interest to their movement, you will use a new patch—**Momentum Scrolling**.

6. Add two **Momentum Scrolling** patches to the Editor.

7. Connect the *X Position* output of the **Interaction** patch to the *Start* and *End Boundary* inputs of the **Momentum Scrolling** patch, and connect the *Output Value* of the **Momentum Scrolling** patch to the *X Position* input of the **Sprite** patch.

   Now when you move the sprite along its *X* axis, you will see it bounce and settle when you stop moving it, instead of stopping immediately. Try moving the sprite up and down, and compare that movement with the side-to-side settling.

8. Set the *Y Position* of the same **Interaction** patch to control the *Start* and *End Boundaries* of the second **Momentum Scrolling** patch, and connect that new output to the *Y Position* of the same **Sprite** patch.

   Now your composition should look something like Figure 7.6 and you can compare the movement of the two sprites. Try adjusting the *Rubberband Friction* to change the bounciness of the sprite's movements. You can add an **Input Splitter** to manage the settings of both **Momentum Scrolling** patches at once.

9. Connect the *interaction port* and the *X* and *Y Positions* of the first **Interaction** patch, and connect the *interaction port* and the *X* and *Y Positions* of the second **Sprite** patch.

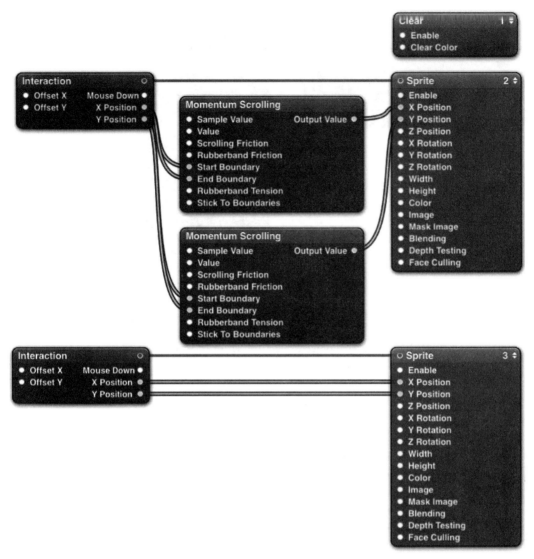

Figure 7.6   The Momentum Scrolling patches put some bounce into our
Sprite's movements.

The connection between the *interaction ports* of the first **Interaction** patch and
the first **Sprite** patch disappears, because each **Interaction** patch can directly
control only one consumer patch. However, because the first **Sprite**'s *X* and *Y*
*Position*s are still being fed data from the first **Interaction** patch, it will orbit
around the second sprite when you drag that one. Your composition should now
be similar to Figure 7.7.

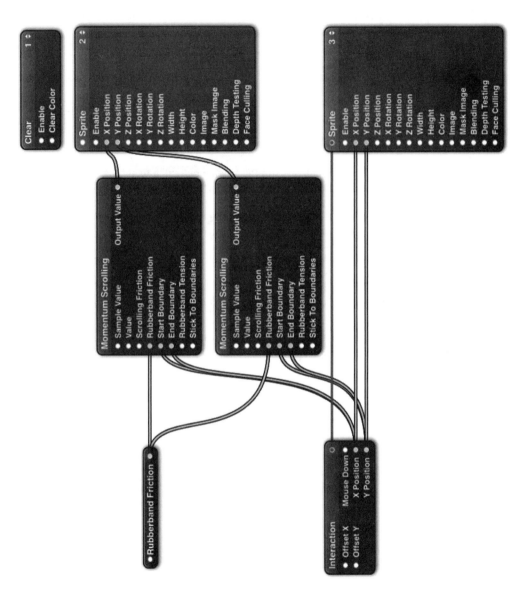

Figure 7.7   The final setup of your Interaction composition, with two sprites controlled by an Interaction patch, and some fun orbiting animation

Controlling a Kaleidoscope

Next you will build a **Kaleidoscope** patch to further experiment with the **Mouse** patch. We will also use **Math** patches to expand our mouse's range of control.

1. Start a new composition, and add a **Clear** patch.
2. Add the following patches to the Editor: **Video Input**, **Kaleidoscope**, **Billboard**, **Mouse**.
3. Route the **Video Input**'s *Image* output through the **Kaleidoscope** into the **Billboard**.

> **Tip**
>
> You may need to make some adjustments to the **Video Input** patch to get a signal. Open the Inspector and navigate to page 2 (⌘-2). Select your video device from the drop-down menu next to "Video Device." This device can be an iSight, a video camera, a still camera—anything that will stream video to the computer in a QuickTime-compatible format. If you can't get the video input to work, or if you don't have a camera to use, you can substitute a movie from your hard drive instead.

4. Set the **Billboard**'s *Width* to 2.
5. Connect the **Mouse**'s *X* and *Y* outputs to the **Kaleidoscope**'s *Angle* and *Center (Y)* inputs, respectively.

   Now when you wiggle your mouse, you'll see the on-screen **Kaleidoscope** move somewhat, but the effect is a bit too subtle. A good fix is to use **Math** patches to amplify the effect.

6. Run both the *X* and *Y* outputs from the **Mouse** patch through their own **Math** patch (via the *Initial Value* input), then through to their original destination. Set the values for *Mouse X*'s **Math** patch as follows:

   Operation #1: Multiply

   Operand #1: 35

   Set the values for *Mouse Y*'s **Math** patch as follows:

   Operation #1: Multiply

   Operand #1: 150

Your composition should be similar to Figure 7.8. Now move your mouse around and witness the changes in your Viewer. Try playing with the numbers and see if you can find a range that suits you.

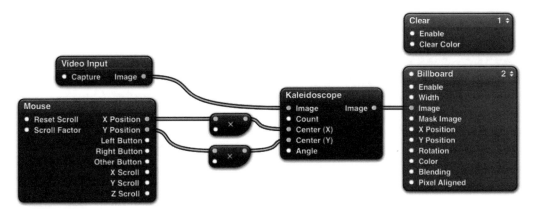

Figure 7.8   The mouse coordinates are individually multiplied to provide controls for the parameters of the Kaleidoscope.

Summary

You've now integrated mouse input in two very different ways. Your mouse provides an excellent means of universal control for parameters in your composition. By now, you should be getting a feel for the modularity of Quartz Composer—how each element can affect all the other elements. Each time you learn about a new patch, you can revisit previous compositions and try integrating your new tool with them.

Challenges

Create a **Particle System** that you can use to draw a smiley face. You'll need to play with the *Lifetime* amount.

Chapter 8

MIDI Interfacing (Getting Sliders and Knobs Involved)

MIDI controllers have historically been used to control audio software and hardware. With Quartz Composer, you can now use keyboards, drum machines, and banks of sliders and knobs to control visual elements.

MIDI Notes

Midi keyboards send out information encoded as "MIDI Notes," which hold information on which key was pressed or released, and the corresponding velocity. Some programs listen for "Note On" and "Note Off" messages, while others—Quartz Composer, most importantly—simply use a "Note On" message with a *Velocity* of 0 to express a "Note Off" message. Remember, also, that Quartz Composer normalizes inputs to the 0–1 range. MIDI Note velocities are expressed as values in the range 0–127, so a *Velocity* message of 127 (the most quickly you can press a note) is considered a 1 to Quartz Composer, and a median *Velocity* message of 64 is seen as 0.5.

Here's an example of the data that Quartz Composer would see if you quickly pressed middle C and then slowly pressed the D just above it:

   C-5: 0.7

   C-5: 0

   D-5: 0.2

   D-5: 0

How to Get the Information

In this exercise, you will connect a MIDI keyboard and learn how to receive data from MIDI Note messages. This first step opens up a wide world of possibilities for interactions between music and graphics.

1. Connect a MIDI keyboard to your computer. If you don't have one but still want to learn how to program for these devices, download the free application MidiKeys (`http://midikeys.en.softonic.com/mac`) to emulate one using your computer keyboard.

> **Tip**
>
> Set the *Destination* to *Virtual Source*.
>
> When MidiKeys is the front-most application, you can simply press the "z" key to generate a C "Note On" message.
>
> Open *Preferences* and make sure the setting for "Keys are system-wide hot keys" is selected. By default, the selected modifiers are *Control* and *Option*; with these turned on, you can let MidiKeys fall to the background and use Control-Option-z to generate a "Note On" message, no matter which program has focus.

2. Start a new composition and bring in a **MIDI Notes Receiver**, a **Clear** patch, and an **OSDebugger** (from Chapter 5).

3. Select the **MIDI Notes Receiver** and use the Inspector to browse its settings (⌘-2).

4. The first option is *MIDI Sources*. Uncheck the *All* setting and find your particular device in the drop-down menu, as shown in Figure 8.1.

Figure 8.1 Choosing your MIDI device from the drop-down menu

MIDI Channels allows you to select which channels to listen to. For this purpose, they should all be selected (dark gray).

Observed Octaves lets you pick the specific octaves for which you want to see outputs in the Editor. It is a handy way to keep things neat if you need to listen in on a particular octave.

5. Connect the output of *C5* from your MIDI Notes Receiver to the *String* input of the **OSDebugger**.

6. Press middle C on your MIDI keyboard; you should see the big "0" on the screen change to a number representing the velocity with which you pressed the key. If you don't see an output, try pressing various C keys on your keyboard until you get a reaction. If you have to go down an octave to get a response, you may want to change the middle C setting in the Inspector to 4.

MIDI Virtual Macros

What if you want your Quartz Composition to react to a C or a B-flat no matter which octave it's played in? I find it wonderfully handy to create a variety of Virtual Macros for my MIDI devices that make it super-easy to use any particular device with a given composition.

Here's how you make a Virtual Macro that responds to any MIDI note, no matter the octave, giving you a total of 12 outputs (C, C#, D, and so on).

1. Add a **Javascript** patch to the Editor. Open the Inspector and browse to its Settings page (⌘-2). Replace the default contents with the following code (see Figure 8.2):

```
function (__number noteOut) main    (__number noteIn[10])
{
    var result = new Object();
    result.noteOut = (noteIn[0] + noteIn[1] + noteIn[2] + noteIn[3] +
noteIn[4] + noteIn[5] + noteIn[6] + noteIn[7] + noteIn[8] + noteIn[9])/10;
    return result;
}
```

> **Tip**
>
> Sometimes you need some logic or calculations that just cannot be easily handled by the built-in logic or math patches. In these cases, a simple **Javascript** patch can do the trick.
>
> The JavaScript in this patch creates an average of all the noteIn information coming into the patch.
>
> The first line declares the function and its properties. In this case, you have an output called noteOut that will be a number and 10 inputs called noteIn.
>
> On the next line, you declare a new object called result, which is like a container that holds all of your important data.
>
> Next, you set the property noteOut to the average of all the incoming notes—all of the Cs, or all the G#s, for example.
>
> Finally, JavaScript needs us to return the result, meaning it should now look in the container and pass along whatever actions necessary.

2. Rename this **Javascript** patch to *C* by double-clicking on its name. This patch will take an average of 10 inputs and forward just one number.

```
1  function (__number noteOut) main      (__number noteIn[10])
2  {
3      var result = new Object();
4      result.noteOut = (
5          noteIn[0] + noteIn[1] + noteIn[2] +
6          noteIn[3] + noteIn[4] + noteIn[5] +
7          noteIn[6] + noteIn[7] + noteIn[8] +
8          noteIn[9]
9      )/10;
10     return result;
11 }
12
```

Figure 8.2   Inserting the code into the Javascript patch

3. Inspect your MIDI Notes Receiver and activate all octaves by clicking to make them dark gray.

4. Connect the *Key C0* output to *noteIn[0]* on your **C** patch, the *Key C1* to **noteIn[1]**, and so on all the way through *Key C9*.

5. Right-click on the **C Javascript** patch and choose Publish Outputs > noteOut, naming the output *C*.

   Congratulations! You've just built a patch that will push the *Velocity* value of any C note on your MIDI keyboard to an output, regardless of octave, as shown in Figure 8.3.

6. Copy-and-paste the **C Javascript** patch, name the copy *C#*, and do it all again and again until you've taken care of all 12 notes. Your composition should look like Figure 8.4.

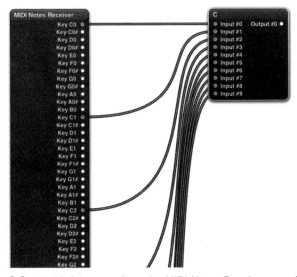

Figure 8.3   All 10 C outputs from the MIDI Notes Receiver are plugged into the C Javascript patch.

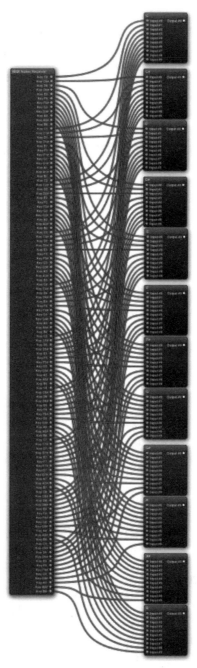

Figure 8.4   All 12 notes are routed through their own Javascript patches.
Tedious, I know—but you have to do it only once!

7. Once you've patched and published all of your outputs, select your **MIDI Notes Receiver** and all your **Javascript** patches, and choose Editor > Add To Library from Quartz Composer's toolbar, just as you did to create the **OSDebugger** patch in Chapter 5.

8. Name this Clip **MIDI-12**. Alternatively, you can use the Midi Notes To Control Sprites.qtz file included on the disk with this book to create your Clip if you'd rather not go through the tedium. (I won't hold it against you.)

MIDI Notes to Control Sprites

Now that you've got your MIDI keyboard talking to Quartz Composer, it's time to do something fun with it. Let's build a composition in which your MIDI keyboard controls an array of boxes that fill your screen. Play a melody, and you get a direct on-screen representation of your notes, as shown in Figure 8.5.

Play the video titled "Use MIDI to Make Interactive Animations."

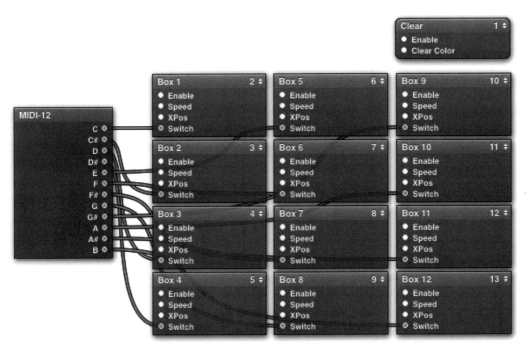

Figure 8.5   The final composition you're going to create—an array of Sprites, controlled by a full octave on the MIDI keyboard

1. Start a new composition, and add a **Clear** patch, your **MIDI-12** Clip, an **HSL Color** patch, and a **Sprite**.

2. Connect the *Color* output from the **HSL Color** patch to the *Color* input on the **Sprite**.

3. Right-click on the **MIDI-12** Clip and choose Insert Output Splitter > C.

4. Use the Inspector to change the type of your new **Output Splitter** to *Boolean* instead of the default *Number*. Note that you must reconnect your **MIDI-12** *C* output after this type change.

5. Connect the output of your *C Boolean* to the *Alpha* input on the **HSL Color** patch.

6. Now press any C key on your keyboard, and the **Sprite** (currently just a white box) will appear and disappear! See Figure 8.6.

   Now you will modify this patch to control 12 boxes, evenly spaced across the screen.

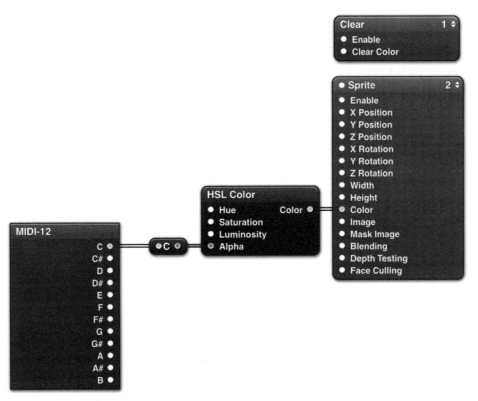

Figure 8.6 The output of the MIDI-12 patch is turned into a Boolean (on/off) value, which flicks the Alpha (transparency) of your Sprite on and off whenever you trigger the C key on your MIDI device.

First you need to calculate a new *Width* for the **Sprite**. Add a **Rendering Destination Dimensions** patch and a **Math** patch to the Editor.

7. Connect the *Width* output of the **Rendering Destination Dimensions** patch to the *Initial Value* input on the **Math** patch.

8. Use the Inspector to change *Operation #1* on the **Math** patch to *Divide*, and set *Operand #1* to *12*—the number of notes in an octave.

9. Connect the *Resulting Value* to the *Width* input on the **Sprite**.

10. Connect the *Height* output of the **Rendering Destination Dimensions** patch directly to the *Height* input on the **Sprite**. Each box will take up the full height of the screen.

11. Now hold down a C key on your MIDI keyboard and resize the Viewer window using the lower-right corner. The **Sprite** changes its width with every change of the Viewer, staying at one-twelfth the size of the output.

12. Add a **Smooth** patch to the Editor, and route the output of the **C Boolean** patch through its *Value*, and then on through to the *Alpha* input on the **HSL Color** patch, as shown in Figure 8.7.

13. Press the C key again to see the patch gracefully fade in and out as you press and hold the note. That's pretty, but we'll want some control over the speed.

14. Use the Inspector to change the **Smooth** patch's *Increasing* and *Decreasing Durations* to 0.1 each. Now a press on the key yields a very quick fade—nicer than a straight cut, but more direct than the 1-second durations used previously.

15. Right-click on the **Smooth** patch and insert an **Input Splitter** on the *Increasing Duration* value. Rename this **Input Splitter** to *Speed*.

16. Connect the output of the **Speed** patch to the *Decreasing Duration* port (so it controls both durations), and use the Inspector to change the **Speed** patch's *Minimum* and *Maximum* values to 0 and 1, respectively.

17. Right-click on the **Speed** patch, choose Published Inputs > Input, and name it *Speed*.

    To replicate these actions 12 times, you will create a **Macro** patch. Think about which inputs you still need to access—in this case, the *Boolean* input that turns the *Alpha* on and off, the *Speed*, and the *X Position* (so that we can line up the boxes side-by-side across the screen).

18. To finish preparing your patch, publish the *X Position* of the **Sprite** (call it *XPos*) as well as the *Input* of the **C Boolean** (call it *Switch*).

19. Select the **Sprite** patch, and use the Inspector to change its blending mode to *Over* instead of *Replace*. With 12 sprites on-screen, you need to make sure they will all be visible.

20. Drag a box in the Editor to select everything except for the **MIDI-12** and **Clear** patches, as shown in Figure 8.8. Click the Create Macro button at the top of the editor. Name your new **Macro** as *Box 1*.

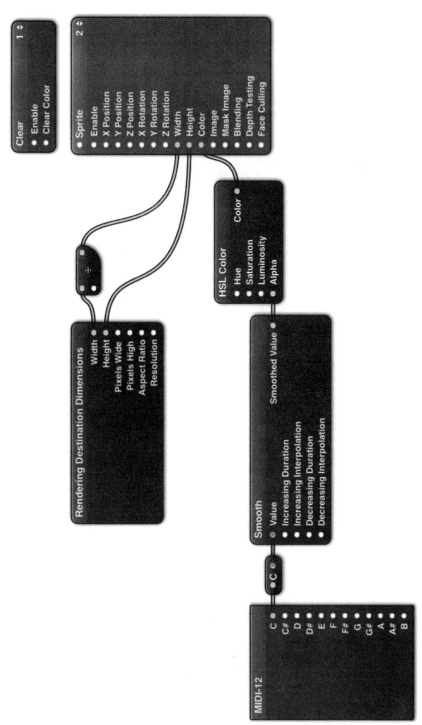

Figure 8.7 The C note is now routed through a Smooth patch, creating a fade in/out effect when you press the key. Additionally, the Sprite's Width and Height are calculated automatically, thanks to the Rendering Destination Dimensions patch.

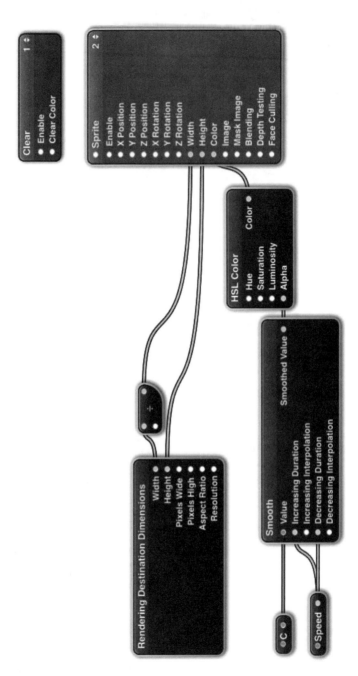

Figure 8.8 All the patches that will make up the new Macro are prepared and selected.

21. Connect the *C* output of the **MIDI-12** patch to the *Switch* of **Box 1** to verify that everything still works.

22. Copy and paste the **Box 1** patch to create a sibling, and name it *Box 2*.

23. Connect the *C#* output of the **MIDI-12** patch to its *Switch*.

    Now you can press C or C# to bring up the box. There seems to be no difference between the two, however, because both occupy the same spot on the screen. To fix this problem, a little math is needed.

    You want to space 12 objects equally across the screen. Thankfully, you've already ensured that each object is exactly one-twelfth the width of the screen, so you know they will fit together nicely. One of the awesome things about Quartz Composer is that you don't really have to think through the math to get stuff looking good. You could easily just hold down the C key while you adjust the *XPos* of **Box 1** via the Inspector until it is aligned with the left side of the screen.

24. Try that now.

25. Hold down both C and C#, and adjust the *XPos* of **Box 2** until it is lined up right next to **Box 1**.

    Using this approximation method, I came up with *X Positions* of −0.9262 and −0.7632, respectively.

> **Tip**
>
> The way to do the math, if you like, is to take the **Rendering Destination Dimension**'s *Width*, **Multiply** it by −0.5 (to get to the left side of the screen from the middle) and **Add** half the width of the **Sprite** (so that you line up the left edge instead of the middle). With this technique, you arrive at the starting number −0.91665, which is not terribly far off from my earlier guess (off by about one-hundredth). Then you add the *Width* of the **Sprite** (0.1667) to each **Box**'s *XPos* to get the position of the next box.

26. Use copy-and-paste to create a total of 12 **Boxes**, naming them **Box 3–12** as appropriate, and connecting **MIDI-12** to their *Switches* in order.

27. Finally, use the Inspector to adjust their *X Positions* to the following:

    −0.917, −0.75, −0.583, −0.417, −0.25, −0.083, 0.083, 0.25, 0.417, 0.583, 0.75, 0.917

Now play your keyboard and enjoy the output!

Adding in MIDI Controllers

MIDI controllers can do more than send notes. For example, you also have "continuous controllers," which are often knobs or faders that output a stream of data you can use to affect parameters with precision.

In this exercise, you will add further control to your MIDI bars by using a fader or knob to control the *Speed* value you set up earlier.

1. First you need to set all of the *Speed* inputs to read the same value. Insert an **Input Splitter** on the *Speed* input of **Box 1**, and connect its output to the *Speed* input of every box.

2. Choose a knob or fader on your device that you'd like to use to control the fade speed of your Midi boxes.

3. Add a **Midi Controllers Receiver** patch to the Editor.

4. Use the Inspector to choose your MIDI controller from the Midi Sources list, or select *All*. Look for the "Observed Midi Controllers" section of the Inspector, and click the button labeled "Learn Controller to Observe." Move the knob or fader you chose earlier, and it will pop itself into the output list of your **MIDI Controllers Receiver** patch (along with the "Pitch Wheel" and "Modulation Wheel" controls, which are visible by default).

5. Connect the output of this new controller to the *Input* of your **Speed** patch and you'll gain real-time control over the fade speed of your boxes. Try triggering them and moving the control to get a feel for it. Your final composition should be similar to Figure 8.9.

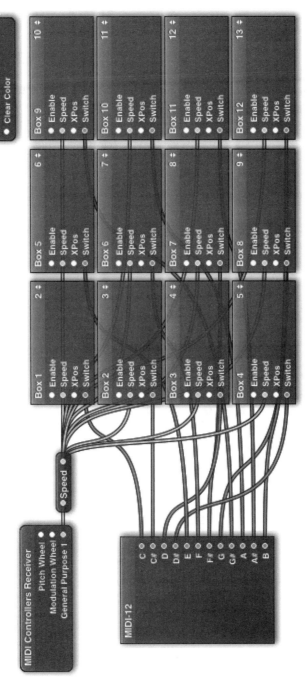

Figure 8.9   Speed is now abstracted to a single source, which is listening to the MIDI Continuous Controller of your choice from your device.

Further Control

There are additional ways to connect hardware to Quartz Composer. You may want to look into these techniques:

- *Open Sound Control (OSC):* This network protocol enables interaction for many cutting-edge devices, like the iPhone, iPod Touch, the monome series of devices, and many more.
- *Network Send/Receive:* With this patch, you can send data in wireless fashion between computers running Quartz Composer.

Summary

In this chapter, you learned how to use the Note and Controller data from MIDI devices, and how to smooth the data to create a slicker effect. You also created a cool macro patch that you can use in your future compositions to get them up and running faster!

Challenges

By now, you should be starting to understand the power of hands-on MIDI controllers for manipulating real-time graphics. Here are some modification ideas—see if you can figure out how to make them happen:

- Make the *Velocity* of the Midi Note presses change the *Hue* attribute of the HSL Color patch in the boxes. (Hint: You have to take the *Luminosity* of the **HSL Color** patches down to half to see colors.)
- Make a controller affect the *Height* of the boxes.
- Make a movie play across each **Sprite**.

Chapter 9

Interacting with Audio (Get Stuff Grooving to the Beat)

As you have been experimenting with MIDI in the previous chapter and listening to music, you probably found yourself twisting knobs or hitting keys in time with the beat. While live improvisation is fun, why not let Quartz Composer (QC) listen to the music and change the values for you?

This can be done simply with the **Audio Input** patch (see Figure 9.1). It allows you to use different parts of the music to control different parts of your compositions. From the simple peaks in volume as a song plays to selecting a specific part of the range from bass to treble, it's all available to you to play and experiment with!

If you are not familiar with terms like *frequency range*, *bass*, and *treble*, don't worry; it's really simple. Such language is just a specific way of talking about the different sounds within a piece of music, if you imagine there is a range from the doof doof beat of dance music or hip-hop, right up to a child singing or a flute playing. Sound works through vibration: The more high pitched the sound, the more rapid the vibrations that cause it. Frequency is just another way of saying the number of repetitions over a period of time. Because bass sound is low frequency and high-pitched sound is high frequency, if we want to make a sphere grow on the bass beat of the music, we connect the lower end of the frequency range to the diameter input. Simple.

Working with Audio Input

 Play the video titled "Mac Audio."

Before we dive into QC's audio capabilities, there's just one more thing to be covered: Mac audio. How do we get tunes into the Mac to control our compositions? The simplest way to do so with a laptop is just to let the built-in microphone take care of it.

Thus, whether there is live music around you or just iTunes playing out your speakers, you will always be receiving an audio input.

Alternatively, you can use your line-in capacity to connect an external source. If you download Soundflower from `www.cycling74.com`, you can be even cleverer in how you route sound around your system; you can pass the output from iTunes to the input of QC bypassing the need for a microphone if you don't already have one. If you are running Mac OS Lion, there have been some issues with this function, so pop over to Kineme and get the AppleScript to allow you to use it: `http://kineme.net/forum/General/soundflowerforlion`.

Go to Open System Preferences > Sound, and click the Input tab. There, you can select and control the sensitivity of your various audio inputs. Adjust the slider so you can get a good range from high to low from your current input.

Our main ally in this fight is the **Audio Input** patch (see Figure 9.1). Let's get stuck in!

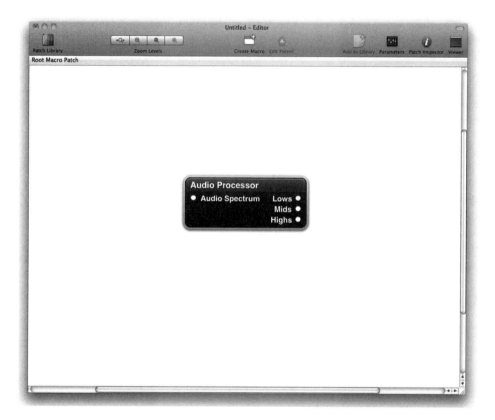

Figure 9.1   Audio Input patch

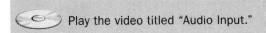
Play the video titled "Audio Input."

To do get to grips with Audio in QC, follow these steps:

1. Launch QC with the starting point composition (**Clear + Trackball > 3D Transformation > Sprite**).
2. Navigate to the bottom level where the **Sprite** is and delete it.
3. Add a **Cube**. Change its *Width* and *Depth* to *0.5*.
4. Add the **Audio Input** patch (refer to Figure 9.1) and connect the *Volume Peak* to output to the *Height* input. Bam, we've got action!

Volume Peak outputs a value between 0 and 1. Assuming you are using a microphone for input, try clapping or shouting. Well done! You have now entered the world of lunacy—people will stand and stare as you wildly clap, whistle, and click at your laptop.

With this simple connection, you can do a great deal, especially if you experiment with this and a few **LFO** patches. However, there are a couple of steps that help with aesthetics:

1. Add a **Math** patch and set it to *Multiply* by *0.5*.
2. Attach the *Volume Peak* to the *Initial Value* and the **Math** *Result* output to the *Y Position* of the **Cube**. The **Cube** will now rise up from a fixed bottom point, rather than growing both up and down from a fixed midpoint.
3. To reposition the **Cube** lower on the screen, add an extra function to the **Math** patch to *Subtract* a value of *0.5*. Alternatively, you can modify the *Y Position* of the **3D Transformation** it is inside.

Additionally, you may not wish for the parameter to return completely to 0. Add another **Math** patch to *Multiply* by *0.5* and *Add 0.5*; this halves the range of the **Cube**'s motion due to the *Volume* and then adds 0.5 so it will never drop below that height. Again, play around with these values to achieve the look you want.

As you experiment with the **Cube**, you may find its movement is too quick, creating a more flickery result than you would like. Thankfully, the other inputs to the **Audio Input** patch help us out:

- *Increasing Scale:* Allows you to smooth the rise of the volume peak. By decreasing the scale to 0.1 or 0.01, you will get a much smoother motion.
- *Decreasing Scale:* Works in the same way as *Increasing Scale*, but controls the speed of the decrease of the volume peak; a range of 1–10 will be quick and 0.1–0.01 will be slow and smooth.
- *Spectrum:* Provides more detailed information about the audio you are currently working with. The *Spectrum*, rather than being one value, actually outputs 16 values, the first 12 of which relate to specific frequency bands.

Until now, we have been dealing with single items being passed around by noodles—images, videos, numbers, and so on—but the *Spectrum* passes many items at once. QC calls these structures. For the geeks out there, a structure is basically an array. For the rest of us, it's just a way of passing lots of information without requiring lots of noodles. However, because a *Spectrum* is not like other noodles, we have to use specific patches that understand lots of values at once. In the case of audio, the simplest one is **Audio Processor** (see Figure 9.2).

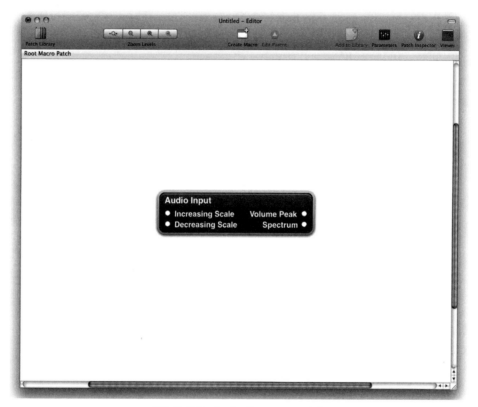

Figure 9.2   Audio Processor patch

Drop this patch in, and immediately you can see that it takes all the values in from the *Spectrum* and gives you a single stream of values from each of its three *outputs:*

- Lows: Bass sounds
- Mids: Main instrumentation and some vocals
- Highs: Synthesizers, voices, flutes, and other sounds

The one thing you will notice is that the **Audio Processor** patch does not output a range from 0 to 1 like the *Volume Peak*. I normally add a **Math** patch to *Multiply* its output by approximately 400. This should be enough for you to let rip on audio!

If you do want to be more specific, you can pull out a single frequency range using a **Structure Index Member** and the following list:

> **Tip**
>
> These are not 100% accurate (Apple has never published the exact ranges).

0: 30Hz, 200Hz

1: 800Hz

2: 1.15KHz

3: 1.6KHz

4: 1.75KHz

5: 2.6–3KHz

6: 5.15KHz?

7: 7.2KHz

8: 9.6KHz

9: 12KHz

10: 14KHz

11: 16.5KHz

12: 18.8KHz

Why not try building a little clip or macro that gives you all 12 bands of the frequency range back as single values?

Output

Having created some audio reactive genius, you may be wondering how you are going to use that outside of QC. Chapter 1 mentioned some of the options, but there is a specific issue with the **Audio Input** patch that must be discussed, so listen up!

Export

If you select File > Export as QuickTime Movie, you can create a QuickTime movie of a specified length and size. In addition to showing you the beauty of being able to create anything from mobile output to HD resolution from one single QC composition, QuickTime will recognize the audio reactivity of any patches you create. For example, if you open the file in any Mac-based QuickTime host, it will react to the audio live.

Or rather it should. Unfortunately, due to a lot of bad noise and unsafe patches, this functionality doesn't work in Leopard. The problem is caused by a mild security issue, but in most cases, it's no big deal; to get around it, you need to rock on over to `kineme.net` and download its Audio tools. Follow the installation instructions to create the folder and then access HD > Library > Graphics > Quartz Composer Patches. Once you restart QC, you will find the **Kineme Safe Audio Input** patch in your library, which you can then use instead of the normal **Audio Input** patch.

Many readers are probably interested in creating a final rendered output in which a composition reacts to a specific piece of audio for integration into a bigger project. There are two ways to achieve this effect: Screen Capture and Kineme Quartz Crystal.

Screen Capture

Using Screen Capture is quick and easy: Simply record the area of the screen with your composition's Viewer window at the appropriate size while the desired audio is playing. For simpler compositions and learning projects, this technique will probably yield satisfactory results. However, rendering at higher resolutions and with more complex patches recording while rendering will slow everything down; if you want the response to be perfect, you need to invest in another Kineme tool.

Kineme Quartz Crystal

Kineme Quartz Crystal allows any QC file to be rendered with motion blur and anti-aliasing. To make it work with a specific audio file, use Kineme's **Audio File Player** patch to make sure this functionality runs along with the composition.

Summary

This chapter was all about audio. Using the **Audio Input** patch, we used the changes in frequency and the volume of a piece of music to control shapes and patch parameters. This seeing-what-you-hear type of QC work allows audiences to quickly recognize that what they are seeing is live and directly connected to the music, which increases their interest and gives you another powerful QC controller skill. Use it wisely!

Challenges

For further experimentation, try playing with the music visualizer template to create your own iTunes visualizations.

Chapter 10

Lighting and Timelines (The Dark Side of QC)

In this chapter, we come to grips with lighting a 3D object and using timelines. We also explore how Quartz Composer (QC) allows you to keyframe animation.

As you have been experimenting with cubes, spheres, and cylinders, you have probably noticed that they look a bit "flat" and unlike how these shapes would look in the real world. This difference arises because, when we look at an object in the real world, it is being lit from many different sources at once.

Even a simple building block sitting on a desk may have three or four light sources contributing to how we see it. Light may come in from any windows in the room, both directly and indirectly, and bounce off the walls, ceiling, and any other objects in the room. There may also be a ceiling light source or desk lamp. In addition, the surface of the desk will affect how the building block looks; a highly varnished finish on the desk, for example, will reflect more of the light hitting it up onto the block. As you can see, the appearance of each surface of the building block is actually the result of very complex interaction and blending of all these sources.

When QC first renders a cube, it gives it completely even lighting from all sides; hence it looks "fake" because it is practically impossible to light an object in such a way in the real world. To get around this issue, you can use a QC environment patch called **Lighting** (see Figure 10.1). It allows you to place objects into a virtual space that contains as many lights of whatever strength you like. Also, a number of settings help you replicate real-world situations by determining how shiny the surface of the objects are and how narrow the beams of the lights are.

If you are familiar with 3D modeling, this material will all be familiar. If not, don't worry—a little experimentation will get you up to speed in no time.

Vidoo Tutorial on Lighting

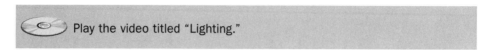

Play the video titled "Lighting."

Follow these steps to get to know Mr. Lighting:

1. Create a new blank composition and add the "starting point" Clip (**Clear + 3D Transformation > Trackball > Sprite**).
2. Replace the **Sprite** with a **Teapot**. (You may not have found this little render patch; it's a bit of computer graphics history and also great for working out lighting.)
3. Set the **Teapot**'s *Scale* to *0.5*.
4. Add a **Lighting** patch (see Figure 10.1) from the Patch Library/Patch Creator.

Figure 10.1   Lighting patch (Snow Leopard)

5. Select and cut the **Teapot**, double-click to enter the **Lighting** environment, and paste the **Teapot** back in.

6. Click and drag on the Viewer window to see that the **Teapot** is being strongly lit from one side. However, as you move the **Teapot,** it may seem odd how the lighting is not changing.

This raises the important issue of positioning within hierarchies, which we touched on a little in Chapter 6 when we discussed where to position the **3D Transformation** versus the **Trackball** in our Clip. Basically, because the **Lighting** environment is inside the **Trackball**, whenever we drag the mouse we move the whole **Lighting** box and **Teapot** about the screen—spinning the room, if you like. Of course, we would probably rather spin the box about in the room and keep the light fixed, just as if it was a ceiling light in a real room.

Follow these steps to modify the lighting effect:

1. Move up one level in the hierarchy so that the **Lighting** patch is visible; select and cut it.

2. Move up one level to where the **Trackball** is. Paste the **Lighting** patch there.

3. Select and cut the **Trackball** patch.

4. Double-click to enter the **Lighting** patch, and paste the **Trackball** beside the **Teapot**.

5. Select and cut the **Teapot**, double-click to enter the **Trackball**, and paste the **Teapot** there.

Now when you click and drag on the Viewer, the **Teapot** spins around but the light stays still.

Let's explain a few more of the **Lighting** patch's settings and features:

- *Ambient Light*: Think of this as the background light. Try changing it to dark blue, and you will see it.

- *Light 1 Color*: This is the color of your directional light. Think of it as a spotlight, and change it to pink.

- *Light 1 Attenuation*: Attenuation is a fancy word for how narrow or broad the beam of your spotlight is. It is normally a good choice to leave it at 0 (full broadness), but you can experiment by pushing the slider up. Return it to 0 before you move on.

- *Light 1 Positioning:* This allows you to place your spotlights anywhere in your 3D space you like. Try changing the Z value to −1 for a dramatic backlight, and then change it back to 1.

- *Shadows:* Turn this on to allow your lights to cast shadows, thereby making them look a lot more realistic (only available in QC from Snow Leopard forward).

Recall that we touched on how shiny the object is, which it affects its appearance. Here are a couple of sliders to help you recreate that effect:

- *Material Specularity:* How white the highlight from your spotlight will be. Play with the slider and you'll understand how it works.

- *Material Shininess:* More dramatic regarding how much white light the **Teapot** will reflect, but depends on the *Specularity*. If you have *Specularity* set to 0, then the *Shininess* is effectively turned off.

Those are the basics. Switch to settings in the Patch Inspector (apple-3). Here, we can add more lights. Try adding one more, and notice how the **Lighting** patch's inputs change to allow you to control the new second light (see Figure 10.2). Find and move its *X Position* to 1 and change its color to pink.

- *Two-Sided Lighting:* It is generally a good idea to have this option on as long as it doesn't slow down a complex composition.

- *Compute Specular Light Separately:* If your scene contains a few different objects, you will probably find that turning this option on will help with the realism of the scene, as it allows objects' positioning to affect one another's lighting.

Timelines

Now we have a **Teapot** with some pretty disco lighting, but doing very little. Perhaps you are thinking about throwing in a few **LFO** patches, **Interpolation** patches, and an **Audio Input** patch, and getting this guy grooving. But there is one more controller object you might just have been wishing for: **Timelines**.

> **Tip**
>
> That's right. In Leopard, keyframe timeline animation was added to QC. If you want to create a complex and very specific set of movements, here you are. This functionality is not as sophisticated a tool as Aftereffects or Motion, which users may be accustomed to, but it works. Leopard users: Timelines can cause the occasional crash, so save your work often when working with them.

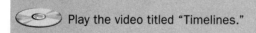 Play the video titled "Timelines."

Follow these steps to learn the ways of the **Timeline** patch, working with your open composition:

1. Add a **Timelines** patch.

2. Connect the *Timeline 1 output* from **Timelines** to the *Y Position* of the **Teapot**. Immediately, your **Teapot** jumps to the top of the screen.

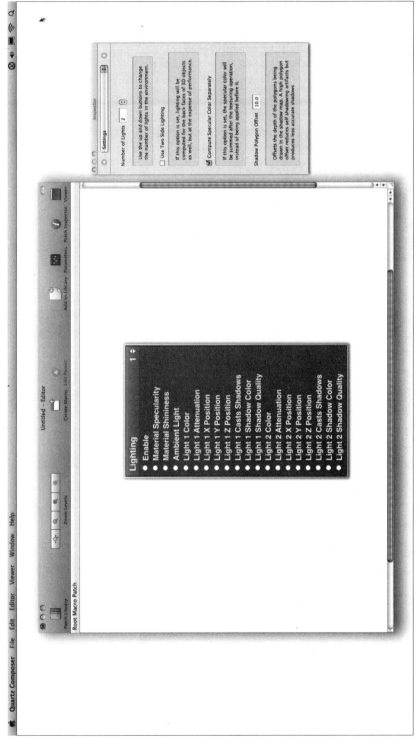

Figure 10.2   The Lighting patch with a second light added

3 To understand this effect, try clicking Stop on the Viewer window and then Run. The **Timeline** starts when Run starts, so it's best used for short pieces that are being rendered and then pieced together in Final Cut or some other application.

4. Select **Timelines** in the Editor and open its Settings pane in the Patch Inspector (⌘-i, ⌘-2) Here, we can see the **Timeline** and some instructions on how to use it. If you have never used a **Timeline** before, it's fairly simple.

When you click Run on the Viewer, t or *time* = 0. As *time* ticks along, values will change with the lines. At $t = 0$, when you click Run, the **Teapot**'s *Y Position* = 0 (in the middle of the screen). As time counts along to 1 second, it gradually changes to 1 (almost off-screen).

Let's play with this option:

1. Double-click the point at $t = 0$ and enter 1 in the v box, or just click and drag it.

2. Change the point at $t = 1$ to 0.

3. Now click Stop and Run on the Viewer; the **Teapot** drops in from the top. That's much better.

4. Let's try *Rotation*. Click "Add new timeline" and call it *rot*.

5. Holding the Control key while clicking allows you to add new points. Add one at $t = 0$ and leave it at $v = 0$.

6. At about $t = 0.9$, Ctrl-click the line again to add a second point.

7. Double-click the second point and enter $v = 90$.

8. This causes the timeline to disappear out of view, so click the "Zoom out V" button above the graph until you can see it again.

9. Add a third point and set it to $t = 3$, $v = -360$.

10. Click Stop and Run. Like the result? Start playing around yourself.

Summary

In this chapter, we discovered the **Lighting** environment patch and learned how to use it to light a 3D object to create more realistic scene in for the viewer. We then learned how to use **Timelines** to control very specific changes of certain patch attributes, remembering that the time in QC counts from when the render to the Viewer window operation began, which can be controlled with the Stop and Run buttons.

Challenges

Try creating a zoom effect in the composition by adding another **Timeline** or controller. Experiment with controller objects and the different inputs of the **Lighting** patch to create a flashing light.

Chapter 11

Replication/Iteration (The Bomb)

Why have just one interesting interactive object when you can have hundreds? By harnessing the powers of replication, you can quickly make beautiful and complicated-looking systems with a minimum of repetitive work.

 Play the video titled "Use Replication to Multiply the Awesome."

Demo: Replicate in Space

The **Replicate in Space** patch is probably the easiest way to multiply your objects. Any object you place inside of it will be replicated, with many controls available. In this exercise, you'll create an awesome-looking generative visual made out of simple cubes.

1. Add the following patches to your editor: **Mouse**, **Clear**, **Cube**.
2. Set the *Width*, *Height* and *Depth* of the **Cube** to *0.25*.
3. Add a **Math** patch, and use it to multiply the *X Position* of the **Mouse** by *90*, and then connect the *Result* to the *Y Rotation* of the **Cube**.
4. Click on the Viewer and move your mouse horizontally to see the **Cube** spin upon its *Y* axis.
5. Connect the *Y Position* of the **Mouse** to the *X Rotation* of the **Cube**, using a copy of your previous **Math** patch to multiply the *Position* by *180* before connecting it.
6. Change the *Operand #1* on your *Y Position*'s **Math** patch to negative 90 (−90) to have up mouse movements translate into an upward rotation (instead of the reverse).

The cube looks very plain without any lighting on it. We could put it inside a **Lighting** patch now, but you have yet to replicate the cube. For this exercise, you want one unified lighting source, so you'll replicate first and light second.

7. Add a **Replicate in Space** patch to the Editor (as shown in Figure 11.1), and cut and paste the **Mouse**, **Math**, and **Cube** patches inside of it.

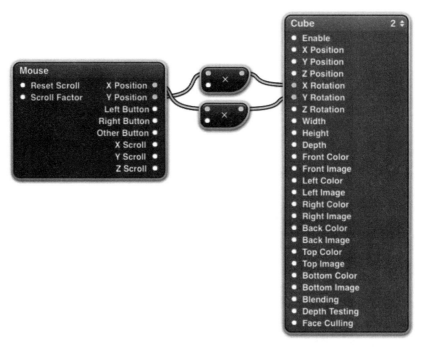

Figure 11.1   The Mouse, Math, and Cube patches are selected and ready for transport to the innards of the Replicate in Space patch.

8. Navigate back to the root of your composition (using the Edit Parent button at the top of the Editor), add a **Lighting** patch to the Editor, and move the **Replicate in Space** patch inside it.

9. Return to the root, and adjust the **Lighting** patch in the following ways (see Figure 11.2):

Material Shininess: 40

Light 1 Attenuation: 0.1

Light 1 Color: Choose any color, but keep it light. (I used an aqua blue.)

Light 1 Z Position: 2

Now click on the Viewer and move your mouse around; notice how the eight cubes on screen move about. Fun, eh? Time to dig in and understand what's

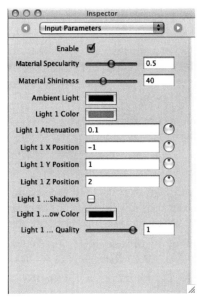

Figure 11.2   Parameters for the Lighting patch

going on with this **Replicate in Space** patch. First, you'll reset the patch so you can make adjustments one by one.

10. Double-click on the **Lighting** patch to get to the **Replicate in Space** level, and use the Inspector to adjust the following parameters of the **Replicate in Space** patch (make sure to try moving the mouse around after each parameter change to see what it looks like):

Origin Z: 0

Final Rotation Y: 0

Now the Viewer appears to have only a single cube. There are still eight of them, but there are currently no differences between them.

11. Using the Inspector, decrease the *Origin X* of the **Replicate in Space** patch until your first cube hits the left side of the screen.

12. Increase the value of the *Final Translation X* until the last cube hits the right side of the screen.

Now you see what the *Origin* and *Final Translation* properties do.

13. Increase the number of *Copies* to *50*. Change the *Final Rotation Y* property to *180*.

Take some time to wiggle the mouse around and see what your composition looks like.

14. Double-click on the **Replicate In 3pace** patch to go inside it, and connect the *X Position* of the **Mouse** directly to the *X Position* of the **Cube**. Return up one level.

15. Now you've got an interesting system of replicated **Cube**s. It's time to step up the complexity again. Add another **Replicate in Space** patch to the Editor, and place your first patch inside this new one.

16. Return to the topmost **Replicate in Space** level (your Editor breadcrumbs should read Root Macro Patch > Lighting). Reset this **Replicate in Space** patch's properties like you did on the first one (*Origin Z:* 0, *Final Rotation Y:* 0).

17. Change the *Final Rotation Z* to *180*. Ooh, that's pretty cool.

18. Add a **Mouse** patch and a **Math** patch, and then connect the *X Position* of the **Mouse** to the *Final Rotation Z* of this outermost **Replicate in Space** patch, *Multiplying* it by *180* through the **Math** patch along the way.

19. Multiply the *Y Position* of the **Mouse** by *180* (make sure to use a new **Math** patch) and connect it to the *Final Rotation X* of the **Replicate in Space** patch.

20. Now you're getting an idea of how powerful the **Replicate in Space** patch can be. For a final tweak, dive all the way down until you reach your original **Cube** patch and set its *Blending* mode to *Add*, which should give you something similar to Figure 11.3.

Figure 11.3 The exercise produces a relatively complex-looking system, which is easily controlled by the mouse. Replication introduces the appearance and aesthetics of complexity without requiring much work on your part.

Take some time to experiment with various properties of each of your **Replicate in Space** patches. Hook the mouse up for direct control and try different levels of multiplication on the *X* and *Y Positions* of the **Mouse** to fine-tune your control.

Play the video titled "Harness the Power of the Iterator."

Iteration

The **Iterator** can do everything that the **Replicate in Space** patch can, and then some. It takes a little more work, but offers greater control and customizability. In this exercise, you will learn how it differs from **Replicate in Space** and how to properly utilize the **Iterator** and **Iterator Variable** patches.

1. Start with the following patches in your Editor: **Clear** and **Lighting**.

2. Set the *Light 1 Attenuation* to *0.1*, and then drop down inside the **Lighting** patch and add a **Cube**.

3. Set the *Width*, *Height*, and *Depth* of the **Cube** to *0.25*. We're going to be replicating this object, and its smaller size will allow more cubes to fit comfortably on the screen.

   You'll need to change the image and color of these **Iterated Cubes**. Here's how to simplify the inputs:

4. Right-click on the **Cube** patch and choose Insert Input Splitter > Front Color.

5. Rename this **Input Splitter** to *Color*, and connect its *Output* to *Left Color*, *Right Color*, *Back Color*, and *Top Color*.

6. Do the same for the *Image* inputs on the **Cube** patch: Make an **Input Splitter** for *Front Image*, *Left Image*, and so on, ending up with something like Figure 11.4.

   Now you can control the *Color* and *Image* for all sides of the **Cube** with single inputs. While it's nice to have the options to affect the *Color* and *Image* of your cube sides separately, you'll often find that you want to change all of them at once. Learn to use your **Input Splitters**; they cost you nothing in terms of performance and make organizing your compositions much easier.

7. Add an **Iterator** to the Editor, and put the **Cube** (and **Input Splitters**) inside it. Return to the level with the **Iterator**.

   You'll notice that the **Iterator** has only two options—*Enable* and *Iterations*. The *Iterations* input functions the same way as *Copies* do in **Replicate in Space**. All of the other operations that were available in the **Replicate in Space** patch (e.g., *Translation*, *Rotation*) are accomplished through **Iterator Variables**.

8. Set the *Iterations* to *8*, which was our starting value for the **Replicate in Space** patch.

9. Drop down into the **Iterator** patch and add an **Iterator Variables** patch to the Editor on the same level.

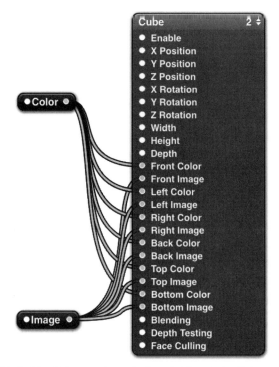

Figure 11.4   The Cube now has single-point inputs for Color and Image.

The **Iterator Variables** patch has three outputs:

- *Current Index* outputs a number assigned to the box, starting at zero. For example, the first cube will get a value of 0, the second cube will get 1, the third cube will get 2, and so on.

- *Current Position* outputs a value normalized between 0 and 1 to represent the current position in the iteration. If you had 10 cubes, then the first cube would get a value of 0, the second cube would get 0.1, the third cube would get 0.2, and so on.

- *Iterations* outputs the number of copies that the **Iterator** is creating.

First you will create a scene similar to the first **Replicate in Space** manipulation you made.

10. Add an **Interpolation** patch to the Editor.

11. Right-click on the **Interpolation** patch and choose Timebase > External.

12. Rename the **Interpolation** patch to *XPos Env* (short for "Envelope").

13. Set the **XPos Env**'s *Repeat Mode* to *None*.

14. Connect the *Current Position* output from the **Iterator Variables** patch to the *Patch Time* of the **XPos Env**, and route the *Result* to the *X Position* of the **Cube**, as shown in Figure 11.5.

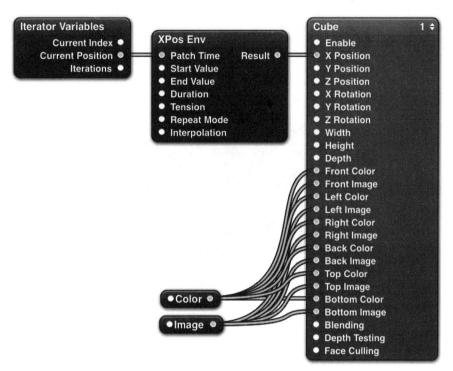

Figure 11.5   Inside the Iterator patch, we use the Current Position parameter to choose a point along our XPos Envelope and feed that to the X Position of the Cube.

15. Now you can use the Inspector on the **XPos Env** patch to change the *Start* and *End Values* of the **Envelope** to stretch the cubes from edge to edge in your Viewer (I used values of −0.8 and 0.8).

16. Add an **Image with String** patch to your Editor.

17. Connect the *Current Position* output of the **Iterator Variables** patch to the *String* input of the **Image with String** patch, and connect the *Image* output to the *Input* of the **Image Splitter** you made earlier.

    The cubes are labeled with numbers between 0 and 1. You won't be able to read any of the numbers in between these extremes, because they have many digits and are being squeezed to fit on the face of your cubes.

18. You can change the *Font Name* and increase the *Font Size* to provide a better looking output—perhaps around 0.25 for the font size.

19. Now connect the *Current Index* output to the *String* input, replacing the *Current Position* value. See the difference? If you're having a hard time reading the numbers, try reducing the *Width* of your **Cube**, so you have something like Figure 11.6.

Figure 11.6   Notice the difference between Current Index and Current Position. Current Position will always be in the range 0 to 1, whereas Current Index will be a whole number, starting at zero and then counting up for each of your iterations.

20. Add an **HSL Color** patch to the Viewer and set its *Luminosity* to *0.5*. Connect its *Color* output to the *Input* on the **Color Input Splitter** you made earlier.

21. Connect the *Current Position Output* from the **Iterator Variables** patch to the *Hue* input of the **HSL Color** patch.

    It's a rainbow! As the **Iterator** steps through the process of creating each cube, it increments the *Hue*—in this case, by one-eighth at each step.

22. Go up a level and change the **Iterations** value to *20*. The on-screen gradient stays the same; you simply gain more steps.

23. Drop back down into the **Iterator** and add an **LFO** patch to your Editor. Hook its *Result* up to the *Y Position* of the **Cube**, and change its *Offset* to *0*.

24. Increase the *Current Position* value of the **Iterator Variables** patch through a new **Math** patch to *Multiply* it by *300*, and then connect the *Resulting Value* to the *Phase* of the **LFO** (Figure 11.7).

Figure 11.7   With the addition of an LFO controlling the Y Position, the line of cubes becomes an undulating worm.

With the powers of the **Replicate in Space** and **Iterator** tools now firmly in your hands, you have the ability to take any of the patches you've built so far (and any you may build in the future) and turn them into complex spinning machines of meta-patches. Remember to keep this possibility in mind whenever you're experimenting.

Summary

In this chapter, you learned how to use the **Replicate in Space**, **Iterator**, and **Iterator Variables** patches. The **Iterator** patch set is a bit more complicated, but allows much more control than the **Replicate in Space** patch once you get the hang of it. You can now take any patch you've made and multiply its impact by using these tools.

Challenges

1. Change the number of **Iterations** to see how many cubes your machine can pump out while maintaining a rate of at least 30 FPS.
2. Change the type of the **LFO** to learn the different oscillations you can produce.
3. Restrict the color of the gradient to only two colors instead of the full rainbow spectrum.
4. Figure out how to spell words out across the cubes—one letter per cube, automatically. Make sure to check out all the tools Quartz Composer provides for string manipulation.

Part II

Quartz Ninja

Chapter 12

Modeling Complex Environments (3D Cities)

This chapter brings together what you've learned so far to create a 3D cityscape that bounces to the beat and plays video on billboards—and then, as an added bonus, we'll fly a camera around. Ready? Let's go!

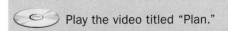 Play the video titled "Plan."

When working with larger environments, it's worth the effort to start with paper and pencil: Draw out a rough idea of what kind of cityscape you wish to create. Figure 12.1 is my example.

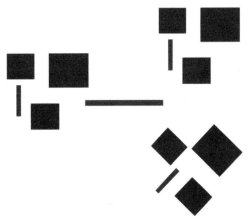

Figure 12.1 Cityscape plan: Squares = buildings, long rectangles = video walls

When approaching this kind of modeling, bear in mind what tools in Quartz Composer (QC) will make it possible. We are going to use **Replicate in Space** patches, so I have created three groups that are the same but positioned at different angles around a central point (origin). In that space, I'm putting a large video wall. The trick here is not to try and recreate exactly the complexity of a city environment, but to include enough variety to trick the viewer into believing this is a city. I'm also thinking about audio interactivity; I know I have the **Audio Processor** patch at my disposal; it will split the audio spectrum into bass, mids, and trebles, so I have three blocks in each cluster.

> **Tip**
>
> If you want to model buildings that are more complex than a cube, you can. Simply use a mixture of cubes and cylinders to get as close an approximation as you need. Be careful not to overcomplicate your buildings, especially as you come to grips with this technique. Too much detail leads to some headaches with the next step.

Texturing

You can probably imagine how you could create a set of shapes like that in our plan. But how on earth are we going to make them look like buildings? We'll use a simple trick to do so. Because all the sides of these cubes take an image input, we use photos of the sides of buildings to "wrap" the 3D cube up.

This is a great time to get creative: Grab a camera (or your phone) and get outside, snapping some photos of buildings that you like (try to get full-length shots of each side or at least two sides). Then drag those images into Photoshop or the like, and crop them so you just have the front of the building—something like what's shown in Figure 12.2.

Don't be afraid to modify the images dramatically. Trying to model very accurately gets increasingly more demanding, so going for something a little more stylized will help create a more convincing result. Before exporting an image for use in QC, consider resizing the photo to something in line with your likely end video product. If your city will end up as part of a standard definition video project, then you can probably shrink photos considerably. Even if the texture fills the screen at some point in our animation, we don't need it any larger than 800 pixels, because an SD frame is only 720 pixels wide. You can leave this setting at a bigger size if you aren't sure what you're going to do with the images, as QC renders only the amount it needs. If your city composition slows down significantly, however, you might have to come back and shrink these texture images!

From your own plan, you know how many textures you need. Remember that four sides of each cube will model the sides of the buildings, but you can get away with using the same image for a few sides. The image in Figure 12.2, for example, can be used for all four sides, as that type of apartment building is roughly the same on all four sides.

Figure 12.2   Cropped image of the front of a building

As you take images, note that a wide-angle lens (like that found on all camera phones and most basic digital cameras) will produce a little distortion so that the sides and tops of the buildings will not be completely square. The easiest way around this problem is to take the best general crop. However, if you want to get the image bang on, you need to use a true lens (50mm) or set your zoom lens to this length; this technique will avoid any distortion. Of course, trying to get far enough away from a building in a city to get its entire façade in at 50mm might be a headache. One nice workaround if you have Photoshop available is to use the lens distortion correction tool. With it, a bit of fiddling about will get you very good results.

So now that we have a plan and some textures, let's start building the cityscape. Video tutorial on!

One City Building

 Play the video titled "One City Building."

The way to make a big environment is through lots of bits that we link together. Let's create our first city building:

1. Open QC, create a new blank **Starting Point** Clip (**Clear + 3D Transformation > Trackball > Sprite**). Delete the S**prite** and add a **Cube**.
2. Drag in the image you want to use for the building's front or use the one in the resource folder called 12RTM02.jpg.
3. Add the **Image Dimensions** patch and plug in your image.
4. Hover your mouse over the *Aspect Ratio* output. It will give you a figure like 0.5, which means that your **Cube** needs to be twice as high as it is wide to avoid the texture appearing distorted.
5. Key in *0.5* for the *Height* and *0.25* for the *Width*.
6. Attach your texture's image output to the *Front, Back, Left,* and *Right Image* inputs of the **Cube**.
7. Use the mouse in the Viewer window to move the **Cube** around the screen. Looking good!
8. The top and bottom of the building are still blank. Unless you have a helicopter, you probably didn't get a photo to use for the roof! One workaround I like is just to use a concrete-texture cropped square. Grab the one from the resources folder, add it to the composition, and connect it to the *Top* and *Bottom Image Inputs.*

Beat Reaction

 Play the video titled "Beat Reactive Building."

Now for some beat reaction! Let's continue with the same wee composition:

1. Add an **Audio Input** patch (Kineme safe version preferably) and an **Audio Processor** patch.

2. Add two **Mathematical Expression** patches. These patches are just the same as the **Math** patch except that they are a bit more flexible and take up a bit less space in the Editor.

3. Use the Patch Inspector's Settings pane (⌘-i, ⌘-2) to set one **Mathematical Expression** to contain a formula [(a*10)+0.25] that prevents the cube from disappearing when there is no audio playing, and the other **Mathematical Expression** to (a*0.5) so that the cube bounces up from the bottom of the shape instead of growing up and down from a central position.

4. Start some music on your system using iTunes, and hook up these items to create something nice. For example, as in Chapter 9, **Audio Input** *Spectrum* > **Audio Processor** *Audio Spectrum*, **Audio Processor** *Lows* > **Mathematical Expression 1** *a*, **Mathematical Expression1** *Result* > **Cube** *Height*; **Math Expression** *Result* > **Mathematical Expression 2** *a*; **Mathematical Expression 2** *Result* > **Cube** *Y Position*.

Macro It Up

 Play the video titled "Simple Building."

We could start replicating or iterating this building right away, but because our plan has clusters of three and we want a unique audio reaction from each building in the cluster, we will manually duplicate this cube. To keep things organized, we will make a macro of this object. You can also save it as a Virtual Macro for future projects.

Let's get the right outputs going the right way, working from the same super-composition:

1. Use the same image on all four sides by using an **Input Splitter** (Ctrl-click the patch, Insert Input Splitter>Front Image).

2. Connect the **Front Image Input Splitter** to the other *Image* inputs—*Back, Right,* and *Left.* Rename it to **Texture Image Splitter**.

3. Ctrl-click the **Texture Image Splitter**, Publish Inputs > Input; rename the input to *Side Texture Image*.

4. Use the same technique to create a published input for the roof texture, naming it *Top and Btm Texture Image*.

5. For the audio input, we want to keep the audio processor out of the macro. Publish the input *a* to the **Mathematical Expression 1**, naming it *Audio Band In*.

6. For greater flexibility, we'll create a sensitivity input. Edit the formula of **Mathematical Expression 1** to *a*b +0.25*.

7. Add an **Input Splitter** for the new *h* input to **Mathematical Expression 1**, set the value to 10, and publish the input to it, naming it *Audio Multiplier*.

8. Highlight everything except the image files and the audio input and processor, as they will be common to many of the city blocks. Then use the Create Macro button on the Editor's top panel, naming your macro *City Block*.

Duplication

 Play the video titled "3 Building Block."

At this point, you should now have one city block macro with four inputs: *Audio Band In*, *Audio Multiplier*, *Side Texture Image*, and *Top and Btm Texture Image*. This is the building block for each of the clusters in our plan (refer to Figure 12.1). Now we will create a cluster from three of these city block macros.

Still with the same mad skillz composition:

1. Duplicate (⌘-d) the city block macro, naming it *City Block Lower*. It will not be visible, as it is right on top of the other building.

2. To reposition this second building as planned, double-click to enter the macro and modify the *X Position* to *2.7* and the *Z Position* to *1.8* of the **Cube**.

3. To help see what's going on, move to the top of the hierarchy, and set the **3D Transformation**'s *X Rotation* to 90 and *Z Position* to –3. This will give you a plan view of your 3D world. On your way back down the hierarchy, reset the **Trackball** to make sure you're starting at the right place.

4. Connect up *Highs* from the **Audio Processor** to *Audio Band In* of the **City Block Lower** and use the same image inputs.

5. Duplicate (⌘-d) the city block macro again, naming it *City Block Bigger*.

6. Enter the **City Block Bigger** macro. Increase its **Cube** *Width* and *Depth,* and modify its *X* and *Z Position* to match the plan. Try to experiment with this on your own. If you are stuck, note that I used the following values: *Width,* 0.5; *Depth,* 0.4; *X Position,* 0.57; *Z Position,* –0.26.

7. Move up the hierarchy so that you can see all of the macros. Add the second texture from the resource folder (`city block bigger texture.jpg`) if you didn't shoot your own.

8. Connect the new texture to the *Side Texture Image* of **City Block Bigger**, the same roof image to *Top and Btm Texture Image,* and the remaining *Highs* output from **Audio Processor** to *Audio Band In*.

9. Have a marvel at your wonderful creation! Start some music and play around with the *Audio Multiplier* inputs to get the city blocks bouncing along in a way you like!

Video Walls

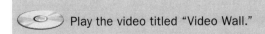 Play the video titled "Video Wall."

To complete our cluster, we need a video wall. As you know, you can put video onto any surface of any shape. So what will we use? The simplest choice is a **Sprite**—but because **Sprites** have no thickness, once we start flying a camera around this will look weird. A **Cube** that is wide and high and very narrow, with video on the *Front* and *Back Image* and black or a texture on the rest, will do the trick. You can then add another **Cube** below it to act as the support.

One little "gotcha" at this point is the floor level. The buildings are all on the same level, as they are duplicates of each other, but positioning this screen can be tricky. Placing all these objects in a **Trackball** helps a lot, but establishing a floor level is what we really need. As with the video screens, although this can be accomplished via a **Sprite**, a **Cube** has the variable depth we need to make this effect seem convincing.

With the same beefy composition,

1. Add a **Cube**, change its *Height* to *0.1*, and name it *Floor*.

2. Change the *Top Color* to red to help see what's going on.

3. Adjust the *Width* and *Depth* to 3.

4. Using the trackball to view the buildings and this floor cube, slowly modify the *Y Position* by dropping the floor down until it is just touching the bottom of the buildings (−0.5).

5. Add a **Cube**, name it **Tv**, and set its *Width* to *0.4,* its *Height* to *0.25,* and its *Depth* to *0.04.*

6. Input split *Front Image* and connect it to *Back Image*. Publish the *Input,* naming it *Vid In.*

7. Input split *Top, Bottom, Left,* and *Right Image*. Publish the *Input,* naming it *Texture for Stand.*

8. Adjust the *Y Position* to *0.28*. Duplicate **Tv**, naming it *Tv Stand.*

9. Set **Tv Stand**'s *Height* to *0.15*, and adjust its *Y Position* so that it looks like it is just touching the **Tv** (0.086).

10. Connect the *Texture for Stand* image split to all six *Image* inputs on **Tv Stand**.

11. Select both **Tv** and **Tv Stand** and their **Input Splitters** to create a macro called **Tv Wall**.

12. Position the **Tv Wall** in relation to the buildings, as we did in the plan (Figure 12.1).

13. Add a video and connect it to the *Vid In* input of **Tv Wall** (There is one in the resources folder, but try one of your own because it's much more fun!)

14. Select everything at the level of **City Blocks** and **Tv Wall** except the video and the audio input, and create another macro. Call it **City Block** and pat yourself on the back for creating your first cluster!

If you want to take a closer look, go back up to the top **3D Transformation**, reset its *X Rotation* to 0 and its *Z Translation* to 0, and then use the **Trackball** to admire your handiwork. Your saved composition should resemble that found in city block cluster ready 2 rep.qtz.

> **Tip**
>
> When it comes to creating macros, you have to make a judgment about how much to put "in" the macro and how much to publish up. The more you publish up, the more flexible your composition will be—but the more noodles you will have to connect to each instance to get it working. So there is always a balance.
>
> In this case, I could have published the building textures and the individual bass, mid. and treble audio components, but for now I'm keeping things simple. A very useful thing is to create a master scale value for the macro, in which a single **Input Splitter** and lots of **Math** patches can be connected to alter the scale of each element of the block and the relative distances separating the various elements. This is a bit of a headache to work out but will prove very useful if you want to create a range of cityscapes from various blocks.

Replicating

 Play the video titled "Making the City."

Now we are going to take our single city block and replicate it twice to match our plan. Continuing with the same mega-composition:

1. Add a **Replicate in Space** patch.

2. Cut and paste your city block macro into it and—bam—you have a bit of a mess!

3. To sort this out, go to the top **3D Transformation** patch and set it back to the plan view we used earlier: *X Rotation* of 90 and *Z Position* of –3.

4. Double-click your way back down to the **Replicate in Space** patch. This is a great time to experiment, but for my plan I want three *Copies* and a *Final Y Rotation* of 270. Feel free to spend time playing here. Try adding a second **Replicate in Space** patch, and see if you can't kill QC with a massive city!

5. Once you are ready to move on, don't forget to publish the inputs to the city block back up from the **Replicate in Space** patch and to reconnect your video and audio.

Master Scale

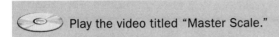

Play the video titled "Master Scale."

To finish, we need to add the central video wall. You may be happy with just a few more video walls of the size you made in the city blocks. However, as mentioned earlier, sometimes developing a master scale input can be really helpful, so I'll demonstrate that technique here.

A master scale input just means that we want to create a single *Scale* input to the macro, which when modified will scale the contents of the macro in a sensible way. The difficulty arises when we have two or more shapes in the macro, as moving and scaling them independently may lead to ugly overlaps and other problems. To avoid this problem, we use **Mathematical Expression** patches to create relationships between the shapes so they work together. For example, with our **Tv Wall,** the complex bit is having the **Tv** rest on the **Tv Stand**, because we need to create the relationship between their *Height* and *Y Positioning*. In QC, the *Height* is measured from the middle out. Thus, as you increase the *Height*, these **Cubes** overlap. We need to add some math to adjust the *Y Position* relative to that scaling. Additionally, we want to work from a fixed floor, so ideally we want the **Tv Wall** to scale up, not up and down.

Let's see this in action. Continuing with the same monstrous composition:

1. Go into the **Replicate in Space, City Block** patch, and copy your **Tv Wall** macro and its *Texture Image Input.*

2. Use the Edit Parent button to move back up to the level of the **Replicate in Space**'s video and audio sources and paste the **Tv Wall** there.

3. Enter the **Tv Wall** macro, and start adjusting the *Width* and *Height* of the two **Cubes**. Very quickly you will obtain really awkward results where things are overlapping and not lining up.

4. Input split and connect the *Width* and *Depth* of the screens, as these will always remain the same for calling the **Input Splitters** **Width** and **Depth**.

5. Look at those two **Input Splitters**: *Width* is 0.4 and *Depth* is 0.04. One value could easily control these two; just add *a*0.1* **Mathematical Expression** to link them.

6. Right now, our **Tv** has *Height* 0.25 and *Y Position* 0.28, and our **Tv Stand** has *Height* 0.15 and *Y Position* 0.08. Turning these figures into a simple relationship is fairly straightforward if we take 0.25 as the base value, 0.25 * 0.60 = 0.15, the height of the **Tv Stand**, so input split *Height* of **Tv**.

7. Add a **Mathematical Expression** with the formula *a*0.6*. Connect its *Result* to the *Height* split.

8. Connect to the *Height* of the **Tv Stand**. Did nothing happen? That's good – it means it's right. Do the same for all four values and then try moving the wheel in the Inspector of the main height splitter. The TV should bump up and down like a single object, yeah!

9. But wait! We need the video wall to grow wider and deeper, too. To finish, I like the scale master slider to have a default value of 1 for consistency. Create a **Mathematical Expression** with a formula of *a*0.25* and connect it to the *Input* of the master height.

10. Input split that *a* and call it **Master Scale**.

11. Create another **Mathematical Expression** with a formula of *a*0.4* and connect it to the *Input* of **Width**.

12. Play with the master scale, and the whole **Tv Wall** object should scale properly! Publish this input, naming it *Master Scale*.

Finishing the Plan

 Play the video titled "Finishing Touches."

To finish this scene, we need to add a believable texture to the floor and some lighting. To texture the floor, you could go down the route of using a city blocks shot from Google maps or similar, or a very large-scale concrete texture. The results I like best tend to come from playing around with some brushes and effects in Photoshop. To achieve the best results, I make a screen capture of the Viewer window with the composition in plan mode. Then, I create a canvas of size 2000 × 2000 and use the plan as a guide so I know where to paint various features. At that point, I start experimenting with different grunge and graph brushes. Once you have something you like, save it as a `jpeg` or `png` file, or use `floor.png` from the resources folder if you don't want to create your own.

Continuing with the same gigantic composition:

1. Drag your floor texture image into the composition at the level of your **Floor Cube**.

2. Attach the floor *Image* output to the *Top, Front, Back, Right,* and *Left Image* inputs of **Floor** and see if you like the result, At this stage you might want to go back to Photoshop and modify your texture to make it fit better. Keep going until you have something that works for you.

3. Drag the `floor 2.png` image into the composition and attach it to **Floor**. Here I added some dark areas to make the buildings blend better with the floor texture.

4. Add a lighting environment to the composition. As discussed earlier, the level of the hierarchy at which you add this environment will affect how we interact with the lighting. I place it at the very top so that all our interactions are "under the lights."

5. Add two extra lights in the Settings pane (⌘-i, ⌘-2) at *X, Y, Z Position* 1, 2, 0 and 0, 1, −2 (or experiment and make your own choices).

6. Turn the specularity down to 0 in the Input Parameters pane (⌘-1) because cities aren't shiny.

7. From here on in, your choices are just a matter of personal taste. Maybe you want to increase the floor size; maybe you think the buildings are a little close. Once you are happy with your city, however, you can start animating.

Camera

The beauty of an environment like the city described in this chapter is that how you use it is totally flexible. With your highest-level **3D Transformation** patch, you can apply any of your controller objects to create a variety of looks. LFO on the *Y* rotation can be used to create a simple spin around the environment, interpolation on the *Z* position can be used to create a zoomer, and a timeline can be used to create something complex. The choice is yours, but remember to save each variation to a different file so you can come back to it. Check the examples and get creative.

Summary

This chapter combined everything we learned in the previous chapters to create something special. Nothing new was introduced; rather, concepts were combined at quite a high level of complexity. Take your time to review the videos and understand everything. Creating good macros with master scale inputs means that you can reuse your work here in many different compositions. Working to create different camera moves is a more creative but very good skill to develop and, if you are rendering out Clips, helps ensure that you get the most use out of all your hard work.

Challenges

So that's it. You have now created your first QC masterpiece. Can you figure out how to extend it? Have a think and a play, and upload your results for the world to see. A few hints: Use addition blending to create see-through elements, put a sphere around everything, and use sky textures to make your world complete.

Chapter 13

Create a Cocoa App
(Send Quartz to Your Friends)

Apple has taken pains to integrate Quartz Composer (QC) into its Development System, making it easy for amateurs to create native applications that can manipulate Quartz Composer compositions. This chapter covers the basics of using Xcode and guides you all the way through publishing an application. This means you can create you very own apps to put on any Mac, anywhere! This is some pretty hardcore stuff, and very closely linked to the operating system. Consequently, we cover how to do it in Snow Leopard and Leopard, and then how to do it in Lion.

Xcode

Apple wants you to make applications for its computers—so much so that the company provides a full development environment on the system disk of each computer. When you installed Quartz Composer, you got your first taste of the Developer Tools. Now you'll delve further into Xcode, which you installed along with Quartz Composer at the very beginning of this book.

Xcode is what the software nerds call an integrated development environment (IDE). A typical IDE provides the following elements:

- Source code editor: Where you write all the code for your program
- Compiler: Translates your source code into an executable file
- Build automation tools: Automates some of the more laborious processes, including compiling, running tests, and packaging things up
- Debugger: Helps you figure out why your program doesn't work

Xcode provides all of these features in a tightly integrated app, and throws in another one called Interface Builder that works alongside Xcode to make tasty Mac interfaces—windows, buttons, wheels, sliders, and more.

Play the video titled "Make a Stand-alone Application (Snow Leopard)."

Demo: Create an Application with Snow Leopard/Leopard

You'll start out by creating a very simple application that just plays a Quartz Composer file in a stand-alone window (great for people who don't have Quartz Composer). No prior experience in making applications is necessary.

Extra Steps in Leopard

Apple simplified the steps for making Quartz Composer applications in Snow Leopard. If you're still using Leopard, you'll have a few extra things to do. Keep an eye out for notes referring to Leopard for these differences.

1. Let's prep an old file of ours. Open up the **Mouse-Following Particles** patch from Chapter 7, disconnect the **Mouse**'s *Left Button* from **HSL**'s *Alpha* connection, and set the *Alpha* to *1*. Save and close the composition.

2. Launch Xcode. You can find it in `Developer/Applications/Xcode.app`.

3. From the File menu, choose New Project....

4. Choose Cocoa Application from the New Project Window, and click the Choose button.

Leopard Step 4

Depending on your installed version, you may have a section for iPhone OS/Mac OS X, or you may have only the Mac OS X section. Choose Application under Mac OS X in the left toolbar, then choose Cocoa Application, and click the Choose... button.

5. A Save As: dialog will appear. Choose a location for your project and call it *First-Particles*, and then click Save.

    Now you have the Xcode project view. There's a ton of stuff here, isn't there? Not to worry—your job is very simple:

Leopard Step 5

First you need to import the Quartz Composer Framework. Right-click on the `Frameworks` folder in the left pane and choose Add > Existing Frameworks....

In the dialog that appears, scroll down to `Quartz.framework` and click Add.

6. Select Resources under First-Particles, and take a look at the listing on the right-hand side of the Project window. Find `MainMenu.xib` and double-click on it to launch Interface Builder with your Main Interface loaded into it.

Leopard: Nibs Are Now Xibs

In Leopard, Apple gave Interface Builder files the extension `.nib`. These files now have the extension `.xib` under Snow Leopard—so when this book refers to `.xib` files, open up the corresponding `.nib`.

7. Interface Builder loads up a whole bunch of new windows. From the menu, choose Tools > Library to view your Library.

Leopard: Importing the Quartz Composer Library Items

First, click the triangle next to Library to view the items inside. Look for Quartz Composer in this list. If it's not in there, you'll need to add it.

- In the menu, choose Interface Builder > Preferences.
- Select the Plug-Ins tab.
- Click the "+" button below the list.
- Find `QuartzComposer.ibplugin` in `System/Library/Frameworks/ Quartz.framework/Versions/A/Frameworks/QuartzComposer .framework/Resources/QuartzComposer.ibplugin` and click Open.
- Close the Preferences window.

Don't worry—you have to do this only once on your machine. Now Xcode will know to show you the Quartz Composer options in Interface Builder.

8. Search for "Quartz" in your Library to bring up the four Quartz Composer–related items. Drag the first item—a Quartz Composer View—to the empty window titled "First-Particles" in Interface Builder (in Leopard, this window is labeled "QCView"). When you mouse over it with the Quartz Composer View in tow, it should zoom to the window a bit and present you with a green bubble with a plus sign inside. Resize the Quartz Composer View to fill the window.

9. Now you need to set the attributes of this QCView. Open the Attribute Inspector with the keyboard shortcut Command-1, or choose it from the Menu under Tools > Attribute Inspector. This Attribute Inspector is quite similar to the Inspector from Quartz Composer, isn't it? Make sure you have selected the QCView in your window (it should be highlighted in blue).

10. Click on the first tab of the Inspector if it is not already selected, and then click the Load button under the Composition header.

11. An Open dialog appears. Navigate to the folder where you saved the Particles composition you prepared at the beginning of this tutorial and choose Open.

12. In the Rendering Options section of the Inspector, check the box next to "Forward all events." This way, Quartz Composer will respond to your mouse.

13. To test it out, choose File > Simulate Interface from the toolbar or press Command-R. You should see a window full of particles that respond to your mouse. If it's not working, check that you loaded the new version, which doesn't require the mouse button to be held down.

14. Quit the Simulator and you will return automatically to your project in Interface Builder. Save your project, and then choose File > Build and Go in Xcode.

15. This will send you back to Xcode and set the Build Automation tools in motion. In a few seconds, you should see your application pop up on the screen again. If it does, this means that Xcode has successfully built your application. Play around a bit to see that things are working, and then quit this app.

16. Switch to the Finder and browse to the folder where you saved your First-Particles project. There are a few new files in here, generated by Xcode. Look inside Build > Debug; you should see an application called First-Particles with a generic application icon. Double-click the icon to launch the app again.

Now you've got a Quartz Composer–based application that you can send to your friends! But there's more we can do—such as exposing parameters for real-time manipulation using Apple's built-in interface widgets.

Demo: Create an Application with Lion

 Play the video titled "Make a Stand-alone Application (Lion)."

If you are running Mac OSX Lion, this is the section for you. You'll start out by creating a very simple application that just plays a Quartz Composer file in a stand-alone window (great for people who don't have Quartz Composer). No prior experience in creating applications is necessary. If you haven't already installed Xcode, you can find it as a free download in the App Store, so go ahead and install it before getting started.

1. Let's prep an old file of ours. Open the **Mouse-Following Particles** patch you created in Chapter 7, or the one in the Lion section of this Chapter's Part 1 folder on the Resource DVD. Disconnect the **Mouse**'s *Left Button* from **HSL**'s *Alpha* connection, and set the *Alpha* to 1. Save and close the composition.

2. Launch Xcode. You can find it in `Applications/Xcode.app`.

Tip

If this is the first time you have ever launched Xcode, you'll be greeted by this: "Welcome to Xcode." You can choose the option "Create a new Xcode project" instead of following the path File > New Project.

3. From the File menu, choose New Project....

4. Choose Cocoa Application from the New Project window, and click the Next button.

5. A dialog titled "Choose options for your new project:" will appear. Choose a name (First-Particles), and then add a Company Identifier (Quartz book or My Awesome Company). Ignore everything else, uncheck "Include unit tests," and click Next/.

6. A Save As dialogue appears. Choose somewhere to keep your Xcode projects, uncheck "Create local git repository for this project," and click Create.

   Now you have the Xcode project view. There's a ton of stuff here, isn't there? Not to worry—your job is very simple:

7. First you need to import the Quartz Composer Framework. In the main window, you will see Particles First highlighted in blue. Below TARGETS and to the right, you will see Linked Frameworks and Libraries. In there is a little yellow suitcase icon with Cocoa.framework beside it. Click the small "+" icon.

8. In the dialog that appears, start typing "Quartz" to find the "Quartz.framework"; when you do, click Add.

9. In the Navigator pane on the left of the Xcode interface, click on Particles_FirstAppDelegate.h.

10. Find the line that includes the following code:

```
#import <Cocoa/Cocoa.h>
```

   Add the following line below it:

```
#import <Quartz/Quartz.h>
```

   This step ensures our app can access the things it needs to run a QC composition.

11. Now let's create our app's interface. Back in the Navigator pane, just below where you selected Particles_FirstAppDelegate.h, find MainMenu.xib. Double-click on it to launch Interface Builder with your Main Interface loaded into it.

12. Interface Builder loads up a new window. From the menu, choose View > Utilities > Show Object Library to view your Library. Click the small black play icon (in a box) to switch the Builder Dock to outline view. You should have something like Figure 13.1.

13. Under the Objects Section in the Builder Dock, click on "Window—Particles First." In Object Library on the lower right-hand pane of the interface, search for "Quartz" in your Library to bring up the four Quartz Composer–related items. Drag the first item—a Quartz Composer View—to the empty window in the middle. Resize the Quartz Composer View to fill the window.

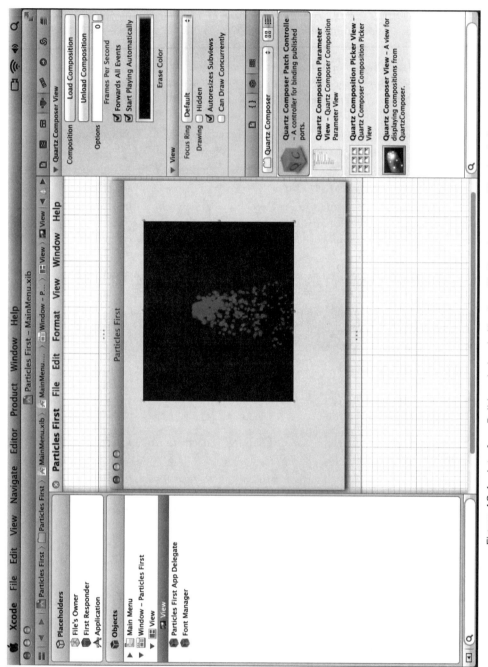

Figure 13.1   Interface Builder window in Xcode, with Quartz composition loaded

14. Now you need to set the Attributes of this QCView. Open the Attribute Inspector from the menu under View > Utilities > Attribute Inspector. This Attribute Inspector is quite similar to the Inspector from Quartz Composer, isn't it? Make sure you have selected the QCView in your window (it should be highlighted in blue).

15. Click the Load button under the Composition header.

16. An Open dialog appears. Navigate to the folder where you saved the Particles composition you prepared at the beginning of this tutorial and choose Open.

17. Check the box next to "Forward all events" and select "Start Playing Automatically." This way, Quartz Composer will respond to your mouse.

18. To test it out, choose Editor > Simulate Interface Menu. You should see a window full of particles that respond to your mouse. If it's not working, check that you loaded the new version, which doesn't require the mouse button to be held down.

19. Quit the Simulator and you will return automatically to your project in Interface Builder. Save your project, and return to the main Xcode interface.

20. Now the exciting bit: Click the big play icon! This sets the Build Automation tools in motion. In a few seconds, you should see your application pop up on the screen again. If it does, it means that Xcode has successfully built your application. Play around a bit to see that things are working, and then quit this app.

21. To share your new application with friends, find it in ~/Library/Developer/ Xcode/DerivedData (use the Finder shortcut of Shift-⌘-G and type this location if necessary), and then browse to Particles_First### > Build > Products > Debug. There is your very first Mac app with a generic icon. Double-click this icon to launch your app. Well done!

Now you've got a Quartz Composer–based application that you can send to your friends! But there's more we can do—such as exposing parameters for real-time manipulation using Apple's built-in interface widgets.

More Features: Publishing Inputs with Snow Leopard and Leopard

 Play the video titled "Add Parameters to Your Application (Snow Leopard)."

Next, you'll use the a version of the **Iterated String Cubes** patch from Chapter 11 (see also the Resource DVD) to practice publishing ports through a Cocoa app. The composition we'll work with here can be found as follows: Resource DVD > Chapter 13 Cocoa App > Part 2 Publishing Inputs > Snow Leopard/Leopard > Iterated String Cubes.qtz:

1. Start a new Xcode Project, making it a Cocoa application as before. Name it SpinningText.

2. As before, add the `Quartz.Framework` to your `Frameworks` folder by right-clicking on Frameworks, choosing Add > Existing Frameworks, and selecting `Quartz.framework` from the list.

3. Double-click your `MainMenu.xib` file to open it up in Interface Builder.

4. Add a Quartz Composer View to your window, as before, but don't bother setting its attributes. You're going to control this Quartz Composer View with another item, called the Quartz Composer Patch Controller.

5. Drag a Quartz Composer Patch Controller from your Library to the window titled MainMenu.xib.

6. Open the Attribute Inspector and select the Patch Controller. Here you will load the **Iterated-String-Cubes** patch using the Load from Composition File button.

7. To set up the Quartz Composer View to listen to this Controller, select it and view its Bindings (press Command-4 to jump to it in the Attribute Inspector).

8. Click the triangle next to Patch to expose its parameters.

9. Click the checkbox next to "Bind to:" and select Patch Controller from the drop-down menu.

10. In the "Controller Key" text field, write "patch" (without quotes).

11. Run a simulation of your project by pressing Command-R.

    Your composition should run in the Quartz Composer View, now tied to the Quartz Composer Patch Controller. The next step is to add Interface elements for our two published inputs: text and rotationSpeed.

12. Add a Text Field (technically, an NSTextField) to your window, underneath your Quartz Composer View. The easiest way to find the NSTextField in the Library is to use the search box at the bottom; type "textfield" and your options will appear. Make sure to choose the Text Field and not the Text Field Cell, which appears first in the search. The Text Field Cell will not be added to your window, so if you're having trouble with dragging and dropping the text field into your window, double-check the type of item you're trying to add.

13. Choose the Text Field and view its Bindings in the Inspector.

14. As with the Quartz Composer View, you want to expand the Value area, Bind it to the Patch Controller, and set "patch" as the Controller Key.

15. Enter "text.value" (without quotes) into the text field under "Model Key Path." This tells your text box where to find the data it's binding to. If you had published your String input as "myNameHere," for example, you would enter "myNameHere.value".

16. Simulate your project again and make sure that changing the text box affects your composition.

17. The last bit of interface is a slider that will control the rotationSpeed. For a challenge, try adding it without viewing the steps!

18. Add a Horizontal Slider (NSSlider) to your window. Use the search box to find it in the Library quickly.

19. Position the new slider underneath your text field, and size it to match.

20. Use the Bindings inspector to Bind the Horizontal Slider to the Patch Controller, set the Controller Key to "patch," and set the Model Key Path to "rotationSpeed.value."

21. Go to the general Attributes page of the Inspector, and change the Minimum and Maximum values of the slider to 0.5 and 5, respectively.

22. Now Simulate your project and see how the slider affects the rotational speed!

23. Save your Interface Builder Project (ignoring any errors for now) and choose File > Build and Go in Xcode.

24. Wait as Xcode compiles and packages your app. As soon as it's all ready, Xcode will launch the app for a final test.

Now you've got an Interactive Quartz Composer composition that's ready to send to friends! Check out http://developer.apple.com/library/ mac/#documentation/ToolsLanguages/Conceptual/Xcode4UserGuide/ InterfaceBuilder/InterfaceBuilder.html to learn more about your options with Interface Builder.

More Features: Publishing Inputs with Lion

 Play the video titled "Add Parameters to Your Application (Lion)."

Next, you'll use the a modified version of the **Iterated String Cubes** patch from Chapter 11 to practice publishing ports through a Cocoa app. The composition that we'll work with here can be found as follows: Resource DVD > Chapter 13 Cocoa App > Part 2 Publishing Inputs > Lion > Iterated String Cubes.qtz:

1. Start a new Xcode Project, making it a Cocoa application as before. Name it SpinningText.

2. As before, add the Quartz.Framework to your Frameworks folder by right-clicking on Frameworks, choosing Add > Existing Frameworks, and selecting Quartz.framework from the list.

3. Double-click your mainmenu.xib file to open it up in Interface Builder.

4. Add a Quartz Composer View to your window, as before, and load the **Iterated String Cubes** patch. You're going to control this Quartz Composer View with another item, called the Object Controller.

5. Drag an Object Controller from your Library (View > Utilities > Show Object Library, if not visible) to the Objects section in the Interface Builder Dock.

6. Open the Attribute Inspector (View > Utilities > Attribute Inspector) with the Object Controller selected. Type "QCView" (without the quotes) into the Class Name box.

7. To set up the Quartz Composer View to listen to this Controller, Ctrl-click and drag your Object Controller onto the QCView in the center. (You should see a straight blue noodle.) When you release the buttons, click Content in the Outlets context menu.

8. Run a simulation of your project by selecting Editor > Simulate Document from the menu.

   Your composition should run in the Quartz Composer View, Object Patch Controller. The next step is to add Interface elements for our two published inputs: text and rotationSpeed.

9. Add a Text Field from the Library to your window, underneath your Quartz Composer View. The easiest way to find the Text Field in the Library is to use the search box at the bottom; type "textfield" and your options will appear.

10. Choose the Text Field and view its Bindings in the Inspector.

11. As with the Quartz Composer View, you want to expand the Value area, Bind it to the Object Controller, and leave "selection" as the Controller Key.

12. Enter "patch.text.value" (without quotes) into the text field under "Model Key Path." This tells your text box where to find the data it's binding to. For example, if you had published your String input as "myNameHere," you would enter "myNameHere.value."

13. Simulate your project again and make sure that changing the text box affects your composition.

14. The last bit of interface is a slider that will control the rotationSpeed. For a challenge, try adding it without viewing the steps!

15. Add a Horizontal Slider to your window. Use the search box to find it in the Library quickly.

16. Position the new slider underneath your text field, and size it to match.

17. Use the Bindings Inspector to Bind the Horizontal Slider to the Object Controller, and set the Model Key Path to "patch.rotationSpeed.value."

18. Go to the general Attributes page of the Inspector, and change the Minimum and Maximum values of the slider to 0.5 and 5, respectively.

19. Simulate your project and see how the slider affects the rotational speed!

20. Save your Interface Builder Project (ignoring any errors for now) and click the big play icon to build and run your new app.

21. Play around with your app to check it's all good. If you want to share it, you will find it in the same place as the end of Part 1.

Now you've got an Interactive Quartz Composer composition that's ready to send to friends! Check out `http://developer.apple.com/library/` `mac/#documentation/ToolsLanguages/Conceptual/Xcode4UserGuide/` `InterfaceBuilder/InterfaceBuilder.html` to learn more about your options with Interface Builder.

Summary

In this chapter, you learned the basics of using Xcode and Interface Builder to create stand-alone applications that you can send to your friends who don't have Quartz Composer and the Developer tools installed on their machines. Perhaps this introduction will inspire you to further explore Xcode so you can discover all the power available for creating your own applications.

Challenges

Create a stand-alone application from the **Particle System** composition you made in Chapter 7, which can draw shapes with particles.

Chapter 14

Create a Screensaver

Screensavers are a fun way to distribute your Quartz Composer masterpieces to your friends, and an interesting medium unto themselves. In this chapter, you'll use the Screensaver template to make your own screensaver and install it on your system. You'll also learn how to use published inputs to create options for your screensaver.

 Play the video titled "Create a Screensaver."

Making the Screensaver

Quartz Composer has built-in templates for an array of uses. In this exercise, you'll build on an existing template to get a headstart on making your screensaver.

1. Start a new Document From template in Quartz Composer, and choose Screen Saver from the Template list.

   This is a ready-to-go screensaver. You will make a few small changes to produce a new effect, and then install it. Check out your Viewer—it's currently showing an example desktop, which slowly cycles its *Hue*. When this document is loaded as a screensaver, it will replace this example image with a screenshot of your desktop (taken right before you transition into the screensaver). You could use this template to create a neat transition into a full-screen animation, or you can directly affect the desktop picture, which is what we'll start with.

2. Double-click on the **Process the Image** macro to jump inside.

   Here, you can see that the composition is simply an **LFO** cycling the *Hue* of the *Image*.

3. Add a **Twirl Distortion** filter to your editor, and delete the **Hue Adjust** patch, transferring its *Image* inputs and outputs to the **Twirl Distortion**.

4. Add an **Image Dimensions** patch, and connect the output from the incoming **Image Splitter** to the *Image* input of this patch.

5. Add a **Math** patch, and set it to *Divide* by 2. Route the *Pixels Wide* output of the **Image Dimensions** patch through the **Math** patch and on to the *Center (X)* input of the **Twirl Distortion** patch. Duplicate the **Math** patch and route the *Pixels High* output through it and on to the *Center (Y)* input of the **Twirl Distortion** patch.

6. Set the *Radius* of the **Twirl Distortion** patch to *500*, the highest number available.

7. Connect the *Result* of the **LFO** to the *Angle* of the **Twirl Distortion** patch, and set its parameters as follows:

Type: Sin

Period: 5

Phase: 0

Amplitude: 30

Offset: 0

Your Editor window should now look similar to Figure 14.1.

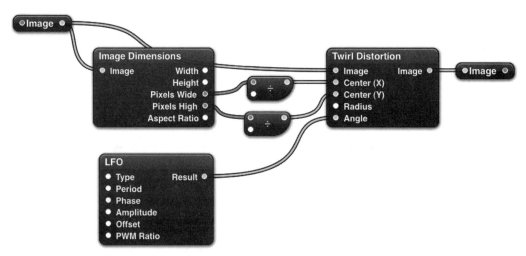

Figure 14.1   The new content of the Process the Image macro, which twirls the desktop picture

8. Jump up one level by clicking the Edit Parent button, and change the **Bill-board**'s *Dimensions Mode* to *Real Size*.

9. Save your document to ~/Library/Screen Savers as TwirlDesk.qtz. On Lion, use ⌘-Shift-G to access your home directory.

10. Open your System Preferences, and choose Desktop and Screen Saver.

11. Choose the Screen Saver tab, and twirl down the disclosure triangle next to Other. You should see your screensaver. Click Test to see it in action.

Adding Options

It's very easy to add options to your screensaver by publishing inputs. In this exercise, you expose a parameter and see how its option shows up in your Screen Saver Preferences pane.

1. Open TwirlDesk.qtz and jump inside the **Process the Image** macro.
2. Add an **Input Splitter** to the *Period* input of the **LFO**.
3. Set its *Minimal Value* to *0.5* and its *Maximal Value* to *30*.
4. Publish the *Period* of the **Input Splitter** as *Speed*.
5. Jump back up one level and publish it again.

   Save the project and check it out in the Screen Saver Preferences. You can click on Options… to see the *Speed* input (Figure 14.2). Set the value and test your screensaver. It works, but it feels backwards. A user would probably expect it to get faster as the number gets higher, instead of slower. You will fix this with an **Interpolation** patch. Return to Quartz Composer.

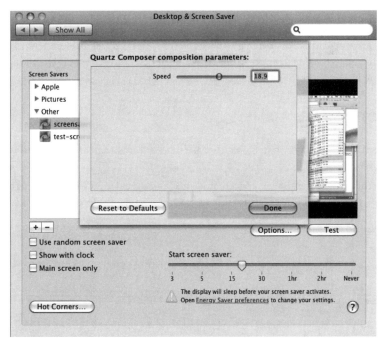

Figure 14.2 The options page for your screensaver, with published Speed input

6   Jump back inside your **Process the Image** macro and add an **Interpolation** patch to your Editor. Set its *Timebase* to *External, Repeat Mode* to *None, Start Value* to *30,* and *End Value* to *0.5.*

By inverting the values—that is, starting with the larger number and ending with the smaller one—you ensure that the final slider appears to function correctly.

7. Connect the *Output* of the **Period** patch to the *Patch Time* of the **Interpolation**, and the *Result* of the **Interpolation** to the *Period* of the **LFO**.

8. Change the **Period** patch's *Minimal* and *Maximal Values* to *0* and *1*, respectively.

This now matches the duration of the **Interpolation** patch. Go to the Screen Saver Preferences again and look at your Option panel. The *Speed* setting now goes from 0 to 1, which feels better from a user's perspective.

Now you know how to make and install screensavers and configure their options. Make sure to set *Minimum* and *Maximum* values for all your published inputs, and use those **Interpolation** patches to make the user interface feel right. You can make screensavers for your friends—just tell them where to install your apps so they show up in Screen Saver Preferences.

Summary

In this chapter, you learned how to create a stand-alone screensaver and create options for it that anyone can access through the standard Screen Saver Preferences in OS X. This is a fun way to send compositions to your friends, and it's easier than creating a stand-alone application for simpler compositions.

Challenges

1. Create a screensaver that shows two particle systems that orbit each other around the screen.

2. Augment the screensaver you created in Challenge 1 to allow for as many particle systems as the user wants through Screen Saver Preferences, with an overall orbit speed being set by user.

Chapter 15

Secret Patches, Core Image Filters, and GLSL (Pushing the Boundaries)

Well, my young apprentice, the sun is setting on our adventure, but if you hold tight to the training you have received, there will be many more great quests in the future. There is so much to Quartz Composer (QC) that we could never write it all down, but we have certainly shown you enough so that you'll be to able to learn the rest and create whatever you need in QC.

However, even QC has its limitations. There are times we need something that isn't available from the premade tools in the Patch Library/Patch Creator. This chapter is about pushing the envelope—there are some extra private patches you can enable; you learn how to smuggle chunks of code into patches; you learn how to access GLSL so you can create custom shaders, use Core Image kernels, and install plugins developed by those people who have created little bits of genius in these areas.

Private Patches

So far we have achieved all that we needed by using the normal patches. In addition, there are some extra "unsafe" patches that you can enable. Be careful when using them, however, because they are not officially supported by Apple—which means when you install the next version of QC, any composition developed with a private patch in might not work anymore.

To enable a few hidden patches, open a Terminal window (Applications > Utilities > Terminal).

If running Leopard, type the following and press Enter:

```
"defaults write -g QCShowPrivatePatches 1"
```

If you're running Tiger, type the following.

```
"defaults write -g QCRegisterPrivatePatches 1"
```

and

```
"defaults write -g QCShowPrivatePatchSettings 1"
```

Plugins

Plugins are the best place to start pushing QC beyond its normal limits because they show us how other people have reworked QC. Playing with other developers' compositions gives you valuable insights into how these bits of code work before you write your own. Included when you installed QC were some of these examples; use the finder to navigate to `Macintosh HD\Developer\Examples\Quartz Composer\ Plugins`.

Here, you'll find a lot of different plugins. To make use of them, you must compile the Xcode projects. Don't worry; it takes only a few clicks:

1. Open the folder `GLHeightField`.

2. Double-click `CLHeightField.xcodeproj`.

3. This launches Xcode. Simply click the Build and Go button, and lots of stuff will happen. Once it's all finished, you'll see a new folder called `Build in the` `GLHeightField`.

4. When you browse into the build folder, and then into the release, your new plugin should be there (called `GLHeightField.plugin`). Grab it and move it to `HD\Library\Graphics\Quartz Composer Plugin-Ins`.

5. Close QC if you had it running and double-click the `GLHeightField Test.qtz` file from the original `GLHeightField` folder.

6. QC launches and opens the composition, which has an awesome 3D shape that is created from the live video input from your iSight (assuming you have one).

Now that you know how to access the examples, you can build all of the others in that folder and see a whole new side to QC. If you do want to create something based on one of these plugins, the best way is to start with the working example patch and then modify it to create what you wanted. Additionally, a number of people online have created some custom plugins that are truly awesome. Check out these sources:

```
www.kineme.net
002.vade.info
http://www.msavisuals.com/tag/quartz-composer/
http://tobyz.net/tobyzstuff/diary/2008/02/
spk-stringtoimagestructure
http://www.audiocommander.de/blog/?p=183
```

JavaScript

The **Javascript** patch was first mentioned in Chapter 8, but it's worth revisiting here briefly. You can add a lot of extra functionality to your compositions if you know a little JavaScript. The following site is a good starting point for more serious development with JavaScript in QC:

```
http://cybero.co.uk/QuartzComposer/QuartzComposerJavaScript-
Guide-Eng/index.html
```

For those of you familiar with coding, JavaScript gives you back all of your **if**, **for**, and other control structures for which you may have been struggling to noodle up replacements. If you find yourself using a lot of **Math** or **Mathematics Expression** patches, it's more efficient and easier to keep track of what is going on by using a single big **Javascript** patch. One caveat is that there are some unexpected inefficiencies, so watch your frame rates!

GLSL

Does OpenGL Shading Language (GLSL) mean nothing to you? Don't worry; it's probably not going to affect your life too much, but it allows you to control how QC and your graphics card handle the processing of your compositions at a much deeper level.

GLSL allows you to do many things, but one great use is to create special effects that you don't already have. GLSL is used widely, so we can also use the **GLSL Shader** macro to incorporate lots of other programmers' fancy graphics code. Toneburst has some great examples at the following site:

```
www.machinesdontcare.wordpress.com
```

If you really want to go deep with this topic, check out the numerous books that are dedicated entirely to GLSL.

Core Image Filters

Core Image filters are basically a subset of GLSL that work with images but offer some custom syntax and options for JavaScript programming. You can use these filters to make some sweet stuff. Although this work does involve writing some code, I promise it's not too difficult.

We'll use the **Core Image Filter** patch to create a new effect (see Figure 15.1).

 Play the video titled "Core Image Filter."

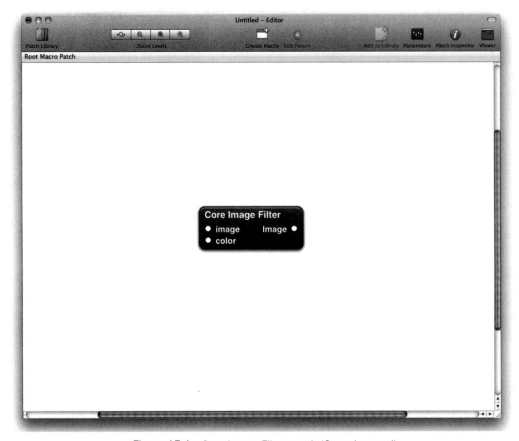

Figure 15.1   Core Image Filter patch (Snow Leopard)

To create a new effect with Core Image filters, open QC if it's not already running. Then follow these steps:

1. Start with your starting point composition.

2. Add a **Clear** patch, two **Billboard** patches, and a **Video Input** patch (if you have an iSight, it works great as a source of video; if not, a general video clip will do).

3. Position the billboards so you can see them both (*Y Position*) and connect the video input to one of them. This will serve as your control, so you can see any differences you are causing.

4. Add a **Core Image Filter**. Connect the output of the video to the input of the **Core Image Filter**, and then connect the output of the filter to the image input of the **Billboards**.

5. Does the video look no different? Great. Browse to `ResourceDVD/Chapter 15 plugins/code` for `coreimage.txt` and copy it. Back in QC, use the Settings pane (⌘-i, ⌘-2) of the Patch Inspector with the filter selected to get to its code window and paste it in. It should look like the following:

```
const float kern00 = -1;
const float kern01 = -2;
const float kern02 = -1;
const float kern10 = 0;
const float kern11 = 0;
const float kern12 = 0;
const float kern20 = 1;
const float kern21 = 2;
const float kern22 = 1;

float getMonoValue(sampler image, const vec2 xy, const vec2 off)
{
        return sample(image,xy +off).r;
}

kernel vec4 sobelFilter(sampler image)
{

        float accumV = 0.0;
        float accumH = 0.0;
        const vec2 xy = samplerCoord(image);
        float pixel;

        pixel = getMonoValue(image, xy, vec2(-1.0, -1.0));
        accumV += pixel*kern00;
        accumH += pixel*kern00;
        pixel = getMonoValue(image, xy, vec2( 0.0, -1.0));
        accumV += pixel*kern01;
        accumH += pixel*kern10;
        pixel = getMonoValue(image, xy, vec2( 1.0, -1.0));
        accumV += pixel*kern02;
        accumH += pixel*kern20;
        pixel = getMonoValue(image, xy, vec2(-1.0,  0.0));
        accumV += pixel*kern10;
        accumH += pixel*kern01;
        pixel = getMonoValue(image, xy, vec2( 0.0,  0.0));
        accumV += pixel*kern11;
        accumH += pixel*kern11;
        pixel = getMonoValue(image, xy, vec2( 1.0,  0.0));
        accumV += pixel*kern12;
        accumH += pixel*kern21;
        pixel = getMonoValue(image, xy, vec2(-1.0,  1.0));
```

```
accumV += pixel*kern20;
accumH += pixel*kern02;
pixel = getMonoValue(image, xy, vec2( 0.0,  1.0));
accumV += pixel*kern21;
accumH += pixel*kern12;
pixel = getMonoValue(image, xy, vec2( 1.0,  1.0));
accumV += pixel*kern22;
accumH += pixel*kern22;

float val = sqrt(accumH * accumH + accumV * accumV);
return vec4(val, val, val, 1.0);
}
```

See the difference now? To learn more, head over to `http://www`
`.quartzcompositions.com/phpBB2/mediawiki/index.php?title=`
`Core_Image_Kernels&redirect=no`.

OpenCL

New to Snow Leopard is the Open Computing Language (OpenCL). The whole idea
of OpenCL is to open up the graphics card to general processing, which increases the
power of your machine beyond its normal CPU limits. The patch you use is **Open
CL Kernel**, and you then write code in the Settings pane of the Patch Inspector. To
get started, look at some example code in the some of the mesh filters (e.g., **Warp**).

Summary

This chapter opened up the world of hardcore coding with QC, for those situations
when a noodle just won't do. Using the supplied examples—JavaScript, OpenGL,
GLSL Shader, Core Image filters, and OpenCL—you can really grab hold of your
GPU and make it do even more complex tricks. The coding languages are beyond the
scope of this book, but the linked resources should be enough to teach you the ropes.

Challenges

Your training is over, QC Ninja. The challenge now is simple: Astound us!

Index

Patch Index

Developer's Library

ESSENTIAL REFERENCES FOR PROGRAMMING PROFESSIONALS

Test-Driven iOS Development

Graham Lee

ISBN-13: 978-0-321-774187

The iOS 5 Developer's Cookbook, Third Edition

Erica Sadun

ISBN-13: 978-0-321-75426-4

Programming in Objective-C, Fourth Edition

Stephen G. Kochan

ISBN-13: 978-0-321-81190-5

Other Developer's Library Titles

TITLE	AUTHOR	ISBN-13
Objective-C Phrasebook, Second Edition	David Chisnall	978-0-321-81375-6
Android™ Wireless Application Development, Second Edition	Lauren Darcey / Shane Conder	978-0-321-74301-5
Cocoa® Programming Developer's Handbook	David Chisnall	978-0-321-63963-9
Cocoa Design Patterns Applications for the iPhone	Erik M. Buck / Donald A. Yacktman	978-0-321-53502-3

Developer's Library books are available at most retail and online bookstores. For more information or to order direct, visit our online bookstore at **informit.com/store**.

Online editions of all Developer's Library titles are available by subscription from Safari Books Online at **safari.informit.com**.

Addison
Wesley

Developer's Library

informit.com/devlibrary

DVD Warranty

Addison-Wesley warrants the DVD that is included in the *Learning Quartz Composer*
book/DVD bundle to be free of defects in materials and faulty workmanship under
normal use for a period of ninety days after purchase (when purchased new). If a defect
is discovered in the DVD during this warranty period, a replacement DVD can be
obtained at no charge by sending the defective DVD postage prepaid, with proof of
purchase to:

> Disc Exchange
> Addison-Wesley
> Pearson Technology Group
> 75 Arlington Street, Suite 300
> Boston, MA 02116
> Email: disc.exchange@pearson.com

Addison-Wesley makes no warranty or representation, either expressed or implied,
with respect to this software, its quality, performance, merchantability, or fitness for
a particular purpose. In no event will Addison-Wesley, its distributors, or dealers be
liable for direct, indirect, special, incidental, or consequential damages arising out of
the use or inability to use the software. The exclusion of implied warranties is not
permitted in some states. Therefore, the above exclusion may not apply to you. This
warranty provides you with specific legal rights. There may be other rights that you
may have that vary from state to state. The contents of this DVD are intended for
personal use only.

More information and updates are available at:

> informit.com/aw